Binding the Wounds of War

In memory of my parents, Ida and Cyril Barnard,
whose foresight in preserving these letters
made this book possible, and to Renate
who was the most wonderful experience of all.

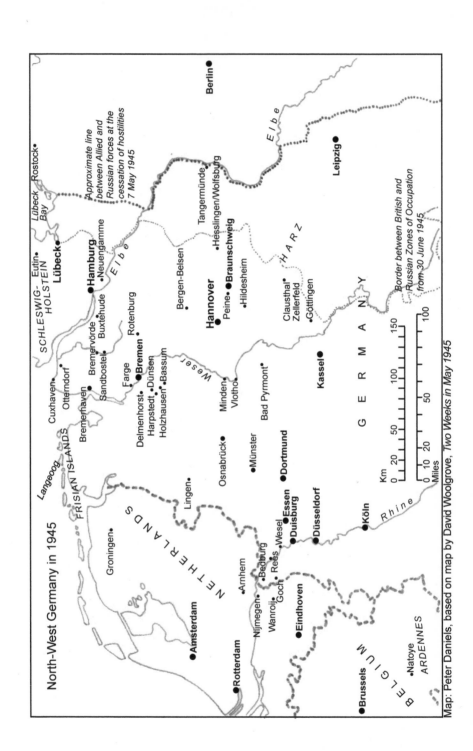

North-West Germany in 1945

Map: Peter Daniels, based on map by David Woolgrove, *Two Weeks in May 1945*

Binding
the Wounds of War

A young relief worker's letters home 1943–47
from the Friends Ambulance Unit and
British Red Cross in North-West Europe

with a revised version of
Sandbostel Revisited

by
Clifford Barnard

Pronoun Press

Published 2010 by Pronoun Press

Pronoun Press is an imprint of Peter Daniels Publisher Services
35 Benthal Road, London N16 7AR, UK
www.pronounpress.co.uk

ISBN 978-0-9556183-6-9

Contents

With chronology tracing my movements at home and abroad from July 1943 to July 1947

Tangermünde: at the temporary bridge (Gordon Taylor)

Tangermünde: the entrance to the bridge. The notice is in Russian, facing visitors from the East, the first line reading "We fervently welcome..."
(Gordon Taylor)

List of illustrations

Introduction

Binding the Wounds of War
and
Sandbostel Revisited

My first book about this subject, *Two Weeks in May 1945*, was an account of the liberation of the concentration camp at Sandbostel. I remembered that my parents had kept all my letters home while I was serving in the Friends Ambulance Unit and British Red Cross, covering some four years, during and after the Second World War. I retrieved them from a rather dusty box in my loft and read them for the first time since I had written them all those years ago. I was able to use one or two in the book, which helped to illustrate events in a way no writing from memory could ever have done. With the book published in 1999 I wondered what to do with the letters, some 150 in all, mostly filled with personal trivia. My family showed little interest in keeping them, which I well understood; the ink was fading badly and the letters written on poor quality wartime paper were yellowing and crumbling away. As I glanced through them wondering how to dispose of them, my attention was drawn to passages which it occurred to me might still have an interest to a future enquirer into this period of history. Would someone, sometime, like to know what it had been like for a fairly typical member of the FAU? Maybe I should leave it to someone else to decide when to recycle them? I then recalled some words I had read from a review of a book by a Quaker relief worker in post-war Germany – 'It is important for us to have these and other personal records of life during these periods of war, persecution, deprivation and stress. It is hoped that other Friends have diaries or letters that will help later generations to begin to understand some of the national and personal traumas that characterise the twentieth century.' With these words in mind I decided to go through the letters making extracts from the more interesting passages and gather them together in an accessible form. This book is the result of that exercise.

The title *Binding the Wounds of War* is a phrase I have occasionally come across in Quaker writing – for example, Ormerod Greenwood in

The Quaker Tapestry (1990, p.211):

> The very fact that Quakers have maintained a testimony against
> all war has often led them to attempt, in however small a way, to
> help in binding up the wounds which war creates.

As it seemed to express so well the purpose behind the work described
in these letters, I decided to adopt it for the title. I apologise unreserv-
edly if I have infringed copyright in some way by using it. Some of the
comments read rather naïvely now, but they were, of course, simply on
the spur of the moment impressions for my parents, and obviously not
based on hindsight or research.

I have been a little surprised to find how regularly I had written,
often weekly or fortnightly, so where the gaps are longer it is probably
because I was on home leave, my parents had not saved the letter, or it
is one that I have omitted during the editing as of too little interest, not
that I had not written. I edited out about half the material as not relating
to my wartime experience – for instance, observations on the Severn Bore
when I was in Worcestershire. I have to admit here that in my enthusiasm
to deal with them I discarded the originals, which of course I now regret,
and I apologise to historians that you only have the evidence of this book.

In editing, I let my original writing stand despite the temptation
to reword some of my more immature comments, although I corrected
spelling and a little grammar, and occasionally redrafted a sentence for
the sake of clarity and readability, but I tried not to change the sense.
Some letters must have been written in great haste or late at night! In
way of explanation and to give continuity to the narrative I have inserted
linking passages in italics. The names of many friends and colleagues
are mentioned in these letters. I did not see how it would still be possible to ask whether they would mind their names appearing. I had few
addresses, most I had not heard of for many years and quite probably
some would no longer be with us. As all the references were kindly, and
from what I remember of them, I concluded they would be unlikely to
object. I found it very moving to recall so many friendships during a time
when we had shared such stressful experiences and hoped they would
also find it so.

I was interested to realise that several occurrences which I can still
clearly recall were not included in my letters, maybe because they were
a bit scary and I had wished to spare my parents any possible anguish.
For example, while waiting our turn to drive our vehicles across the
Rhine over a rather unnerving pontoon bridge, we had to spend a night
in tents. A piece of shell shrapnel passed through the wall of the tent I

was sleeping in and lodged in the cover of a pocket medical dictionary in the kit bag I was using as a pillow, inches from my head! It did not wake me up and I only discovered what had happened with some alarm in the morning. The dictionary with a jagged hole in the cover still sits, with its memories, on my bookshelf.

The letters take a lot for granted and tell little of my background, so for those interested I have included a section giving a little on where I came from and how I became a conscientious objector. To comply with British Army censorship it was not allowed to include place names, but I have been able to add these from memory and research. Reference to the map at the front of the book should enable readers to follow my movements. None of the photographs were taken by me; the British Army had forbidden the carrying of cameras but somehow George Champion, a member of the FAU team, had managed to have one and most of the early photos were taken by him. I gratefully acknowledge his permission to include them. There are also photos by Gordon Taylor, and some while I was in the British Red Cross by Dennis Berry. Otherwise I have no record of who took them. I apologise to photographers I have been unable to acknowledge. If you have any further information, please contact the publisher, Pronoun Press. I would particularly like to thank Peter Daniels for all his very helpful comments and for seeing the book so carefully through the press.

In 1999 during the months following the publication of *Two Weeks in May 1945* I received numerous appreciative letters. Some from people who had been at Sandbostel and through the book relived their experiences, often providing information that I had not discovered during my researches. I was often moved by their personal stories which would have added so much to the book and I felt I had to make this additional material available in a follow up booklet *Sandbostel Revisited*. This was published privately in 2001 with only a small print run and was soon unavailable, so when it was decided to publish my letters home in book form, it seemed an opportunity to include a revised edition of it, and so make these further experiences available to a wider readership.

My Background

I was born in 1925 in north London, but when I was two years old my parents moved to Welwyn, attracted by the concept of the Garden City movement. Following severe pleurisy as a young man my father had been left with only one working lung, a disability that classed him as medically unfit for military service and mercifully spared him the horrors of the trenches in the First World War. Deeply affected by the sense-less slaughter of millions of young men my parents became interested in the beliefs of the Religious Society of Friends, which they joined in the 1920s. They provided a very happy, caring and loving home, where I assimilated much of their liberal outlook on life, particularly their aware-ness for the needs of others in the world. My father was a medical librar-ian and my mother a VAD nurse for many years. They were concerned that my sister and I should have a 'whole' education, and sent us to St Christopher School in Letchworth: known as one of the 'progressives', it was both co-educational and vegetarian. The heads were a Quaker cou-ple, Lyn and Eleanor Harris. Lyn had been a conscientious objector in the First World War, and his older brother Sewell had been one of the group taken out to France to be shot, and only reprieved at the last minute fol-lowing questions in the House of Commons. Lyn Harris's weekly talk on current affairs to senior pupils, and the general way lessons were taught, encouraged us children to take an interest in the world and be socially aware. The teachers were generally kind and helpful, often becoming known on first name terms. It was very democratic and the children had a say in how the school was run, through a council and school meeting. I was happy and readily absorbed the prevailing air of tolerance. The few children of different ethnic origin and several Jewish refugee children from Nazi Germany were treated no differently. I made many friends, some for life.

As the time approached for my call-up for military service I realised an important decision had to be made. I had been greatly influenced by Vera Brittain's book *Humiliation with Honour*, where she explained her atti-tude to war in a series of letters to her son and daughter, who had been evacuated to Canada. I knew my parents' view was that war was incon-sistent with the way Jesus had lived his life, and I was aware of the historic Quaker peace testimony with its long heritage of witness to peace and reconciling diplomacy. I had read with admiration the writings of several Friends who had tried to live in 'that life and power that takes away the occasion of all war', as George Fox had put it in his journal*. For them pacifism was not a negative attitude of simply being against war, but was a whole way of living that avoided contributing in any way, or getting into situations where military force seemed the only solution. I came to see that if one believed that there were alternative ways to war then it had to start somewhere, and I finally came to register as a conscientious objector. I did not find it easy, going against the prevailing views of my peer group, and

The Journal of George Fox, ed. John Nickalls (1952), p.65; the entry is for 1651.

I can recall many vigorous arguments, mostly good-natured, but in the end I felt I could do no other. Shortly after my 18th birthday I went before a tribunal held at Bloomsbury County Court, where a judge and two lay-men directed searching questions at me. It was a difficult occasion. The applications of the two before me were rejected and it looked as though they were heading for prison. However, to my relief, after a short consul-tation my application to be exempted from military service was granted, providing that I undertook full-time hospital or ambulance work. Their decision allowed me to fulfil my wish to join the Friends Ambulance Unit, whose exploits I had followed with great interest.

At the time I did not think too much about it, tending to accept it almost as a right, but I came to recognise that this decision said a lot for the democratic society in Britain, when at a desperate time of total war and national survival, allowance could still be made for those who felt they could not kill their fellow men. The extracts from my letters shed some light on the avalanche of events which occurred in the next four years, some of unimaginable human tragedy, and often following each other so swiftly that I was not always able to take in what was happening. At times I did feel overwhelmed, when what we were able to accomplish seemed so inadequate. However, the training we had received generally stood us in good stead and we coped as best we could. I realise now that many of these experiences, pushed to the back of my mind and appar-ently forgotten, had in fact been assimilated and came to influence many of the attitudes I formed in later life. Readers may find that these extracts from my letters add another dimension to the experiences described in my book *Two Weeks in May 1945*, and wish to read them conjointly.

The Friends Ambulance Unit (FAU) and the Friends Relief Service (FRS)

A word of explanation may be helpful to those readers who are mystified by the reference in these letters to *two* Quaker organisations which both appeared to be undertaking similar work. What may be seen by others as simply Quaker work, is really of two kinds. Those activities with which the whole Religious Society of Friends can unite are organised through central departments and committees and become the corporate and offi-cial expression of the Society's life. There have, over the years, been many other pieces of work initiated and sponsored by individual Friends or groups of Friends for which the Society did not take official responsibil-ity for one reason or another. The Friends Ambulance Unit was in this latter category, while the Friends Relief Service was an official body.

The FAU was first established at the start of the First World War (1914–1918) by a group of Quakers. It was self-governing and constitutionally and financially independent of the Religious Society of Friends, although taking the name 'Friends' and following a general Quaker line. It was therefore free to make its own arrangements with military authorities and in effect became a form of alternative service for conscientious objectors, gathering in the process numbers of non-Quakers. They ran hospitals in France and Belgium, worked on hospital trains and ships and helped to meet the emergency needs of civilians and refugees. It was laid down in 1919.

In 1939 with war clouds gathering again and talk of compulsory military service being introduced, a committee of FAU members from the First World War was set up and the FAU re-established for men of military age who 'shared the Quaker view of peace and war'. During the following six years five thousand men applied to join, of whom 1300 were accepted. Seventeen lost their lives while serving. From 1941 women were welcomed and by 1945 ninety-seven had served. As before, Unit members formed their own administration, raised their own funds and made their own decisions on what work should be undertaken. Although relations with official bodies of the Society of Friends were good there was some criticism from individual Quakers concerned about the Unit's relations with the military and the wearing of khaki uniform in war zones while using the title 'Friends'. They felt that the witness of those conscientious objectors who took a more absolutist stance could be compromised. Early in the war an agreement had been reached with the military that members of the FAU would wear khaki battledress with a distinctive blue shoulder flash and beret badge to aid identification in war zones. The FRS, however, wishing to make what they thought would be a stronger witness, felt unable to accept a similar arrangement. With the Allied invasion of Europe in 1944, FRS were keen to undertake relief work in Germany but there were two difficulties – the wearing of khaki uniform, and having to abide by the British Government's non-fraternisation order. Eventually it proved possible to agree with the authorities that FRS personnel could wear a distinctive *grey* battledress, and by the time FRS teams were already working in France and Holland and about to go into Germany, the non-fraternisation order had been rescinded. The FAU teams, being already in the field before the order was made, quietly took a pragmatic approach; communicating with and carrying German people in their vehicles as the work required, an attitude the military chose to ignore. The order was always difficult to police, and as British personnel became increasingly involved in day to day affairs with German people it seemed less meaningful and was dropped a few months later.

The British Army came to appreciate the contribution the FAU made to civilian relief work and as General Sir Miles Dempsey, Commander of the 2nd Army, acknowledged at the end of hostilities, when he wrote to Major Geneeral Templar, Director of Military Government 21st Army Group:

> I would be grateful if you would convey to the appropriate author-ities my grateful thanks for the splendid work of FAU teams with the 2nd Army. Not only have they been invaluable, they also had the great merit of being available when they were needed. They have filled a gap in our organisation with the greatest cheerfulness and efficiency. No hardship has been too great and no work too hard for them. They have fitted in admirably to our relief organi-sation. If we had to repeat the Normandy landing I would ask for more and land them earlier. In particular I give high praise to the FAU teams who have been with us since the bridgehead days with Corps Refugee Dets. What they do not know about handling refu-gees is not worth knowing.*

In the event the work of the FAU and FRS developed differently. The FAU being in the field while fighting was in progress was essentially a 'first aid' operation, moving from one emergency to another as the need arose, whereas FRS coming later into more stable situations faced longer term problems, usually staying in the same area for some time which enabled close and rewarding relations to be established. Members of the FAU teams were all registered conscientious objectors of military age, and most wished to return to their civilian occupations as soon as the conditions of their tribunal had been met. As demobilisation took effect and members departed, it became impossible to maintain the work and the Unit closed in 1946, handing over most of their work to other bod-ies. A few of the younger members, still with tribunal commitments to fulfil, transferred to these organisations – mostly the FAU Post War Serv-ice, Friends Relief Service and the British Red Cross. FRS members came from a wider range of men and women, mostly members of the Society of Friends, prepared to commit to working for specific periods. Many had special abilities suited to the longer term measures required.

*I only have a handwritten note, copied from an official letter or memo at the time, but there is a similar message from Major General Templar in the British Red Cross magazine *Over to You* (no.2, August 1945).

There was close co-operation with work in this country, particularly in air raid shelters in London and other cities during the blitz and running rest centres for bombed-out families, and in 1942 the Home section of the FAU merged with the official Friends War Victims Committee to form the Friends War Relief Service, later to be known as the Friends Relief Service. The main focus of FAU work, however, was always abroad, and as the war spread world wide FAU teams became widely dispersed. By the end of 1946 overseas sections had served in Austria, Belgium, Finland, Germany, Greece, Italy, the Netherlands, Norway, Yugoslavia, Egypt, Ethiopia, Lebanon, Libya, Syria, Tunisia, China and India. The work had included medical and surgical teams with British and Free French forces in various war zones, medical work in Ethiopia and Syria, driving medical supplies in China (including the notorious Burma Road), relief work during famine and floods in Bengal, and relief and refugee work in Europe. The work of the FAU teams in North-West Europe is admirably summed up by Tegla Davies in his book *Friends Ambulance Unit: the story of the FAU in the Second World War 1939-1946* (Allen & Unwin, 1947, now out of print):

> The Unit's purpose in Germany had been three-fold: to devote all its available resources and experience to the urgent task of emergency relief; to demonstrate to the authorities many, of whom were at first sceptical, the value of voluntary effort in filling obvious gaps in official plans; and to pave the way for the later activities of the Society of Friends. In the three directions it had achieved some measure of success.

A more recent book is *Pacifists in Action: The experience of the Friends Ambulance Unit in the Second World War* by Lyn Smith (Sessions, 1998); and for further reading see the Bibliography, pp.192–94.

In 1947, through its representative bodies, the American Friends Service Committee and the Friends Service Council of London, the Religious Society of Friends was awarded the Nobel Peace Prize. Although not specifically mentioned it was generally accepted that the contribution of the FAU was included along with all the other work of the Society for peace and reconciliation.

1. Training and hospital work

February to November 1943

'Arundale', St Christopher School, Letchworth, Herts.,
18 February 1943
Among my mail this morning was a small brown envelope with OHMS in big black letters across the top. Yes, it was my tribunal papers, on my birthday at that. They don't lose much time do they? It will be at Bloomsbury County Court, Great Portland Street, London on February 24th at 1.45pm. I have a promise of a letter from Mr Harris *[the headmaster]* and have also written to Michael Cadbury at the FAU HQ. For my third letter I think you said you would approach Mr Pettigrew *[in the event my father arranged for a letter from Mr George Lindgren, a local councillor]*, and one from you, Dad, would help. Reg *[Middleton, a close school friend]* had his tribunal last Monday and passed with the condition of joining the FAU, he had a letter from a friend, Arthur Lloyd, who you may remember is an operational pilot in the RAF *[Later killed in a flying accident]...*

It is a wonderful day today for my birthday, not too hot, not too cold, with an almost cloudless blue sky. The hedgerows are just beginning to bud, and crocuses opening up, and if you know where to look, little fragile violets. As I sit here on the old wooden bench overlooking the green carpet of the school playing field, which Freda *[my sister]* will remember so well, I recall some lines of Wordsworth which so aptly describe my thoughts –

> Through primrose tufts, in that green bower,
> The periwinkle trailed its wreaths;
> And 'tis my faith that every flower
> enjoys the air it breathes.

> The birds around me hopped and played,
> their thoughts I cannot measure –
> But the least motion which they made,
> It seemed a thrill of pleasure.

The budding twigs spread out their fan
To catch the breezy air;
And I must think, do all I can,
That there was pleasure there.

If this belief from heaven be sent,
If such be Nature's holy plan,
Have I not reason to lament
What man has made of man?

There are two further verses but I can't remember them just now…

I passed my Tribunal, which I have written about in the Introduction (page 17) and was given exemption from military service provided I undertook full-time hospital or ambulance work. I was given permission to stay on at school to complete my Higher School Certificate exams but had to be fulfilling the conditions of the Tribunal within two weeks of their completion. I left school on the 29th of July but as there was not to be an FAU training camp till October I filled in the time by joining a group of conscientious objectors who were working as orderlies at Winford Hospital, near Bristol.

Emergency Hospital, Winford, near Bristol, 9 August 1943

Just a line to let you know I have arrived safely. Despite a very packed train, David *[Curtis]* and I just managed to bag the last remaining seats, many had to stand in the corridor. The train was rather late into Bristol and we missed the bus so had to wait until 6.30pm for another. David is a few months older than me, quite tall, and went to Dulwich College, where, like me, he has just finished his Higher School Certificate.

The quarters here seem quite reasonable, and the chaps, about eleven, are a friendly bunch. One went to Saffron Walden *[one of the Friends' schools]*, and a likeable, small chap, from the East End, without a secondary education, but a convinced pacifist, who acts as a sort of houseboy.

I started work this morning at 6.30am with a chap to show me the ropes, by scrubbing lavatory floors, and then emptying a series of waste buckets. Then the ward floor had to be polished, with a heavy long-handled mop which meant one had to be careful not to knock the 30 beds, it took a good half hour, but on alternate days it has to be polished as well! There are 12 soldiers on the ward, mostly with broken legs. Another came in this morning and I had to help carry the stretcher and get him into bed. The rest of the time was spent fetching milk and food supplies, washing more floors in the kitchen and bathrooms, and doing the washing up after meals, piles of it! The Sister is a bit of terror and has already ticked me off, but Stuart *[Walters]*, the team leader, says she is only striking while the iron is hot, as it were, and usually cools off later...

Emergency Hospital, Winford, near Bristol, 18 August 1943

Thanks so much for the books. I have wanted to read *Destination Chung-king*, ever since it was published. During my last week at school Mr Harris *[the headmaster]* read a passage or two from it at morning talk, which expressed the greatness that comes from the simpleness of people, who are that part of a nation which matter – 'the common man'. The Chinese coolie, who is the manpower of China – the words used separately 'man' and 'power'. They keep all of life going, and the author *[Han Suyin]* would make the despised word 'coolie' a name of honour, and wrote 'They go by in a slow dream the unaccounted millions, coming out of the mist and going into the mist.'

Winford Hospital is some seven miles south of Bristol on a slight hill, and the city can just be seen in the distance, and in a different direction a fine view of the Mendips. The hospital is on its own – the village being about a mile away, with only one shop, the inevitable 'all purpose post-office-come-corner-shop', it does however have a cattle market. Being 450ft up the hospital gets a steady breeze from the west – I'm sure I can smell the Atlantic! The hospital is in two parts – the original orthopaedic hospital, with a children's section, and the wartime-constructed emergency hospital, which has two male civilian wards, one military ward, and one female ward (military and civilian). Each ward has its own kitchen and utility rooms but uses the theatres, dispensary, mortuary, chapel, bakery, laundry, etc. of the main hospital. I work mainly in the military ward, which has 30 beds, although at present there are only 22 patients, all soldiers, no sailors or airmen. Mostly the result of local accidents, although there are five who were wounded in North Africa. Yesterday I threw away a leg plaster that had been put on two weeks previously in Tunisia. They are all surprisingly cheerful and easy to talk to. Five of them are despatch riders who have had motor bike accidents.

As I said in my last letter the work is mainly chores starting at 6.30am scrubbing lavatory floors (I find it a great time for deep philosophic thought!) and emptying waste buckets. Then fetching the ward breakfasts from the main kitchen. I return to our quarters at 7.30am for my own breakfast, half an hour. The morning is spent waxing and polishing the ward floor, fetching milk and food supplies from the main hospital, and taking prescriptions to the Dispensary, and cleaning the ward kitchen. After a coffee break more floor cleaning – bathrooms, sluice and linen rooms, corridor and so on. After fetching more supplies and the dinners from the main kitchen I work there for about an hour – washing up, mincing meat, etc. At 1.30pm dinner in our own quarters, with the afternoon free – sleep, read, going out, etc. Tea at 5.00pm and then back to the ward – fetching night milk, dispensaries and surgical packs *[for dressings]* from the theatre block on a special trolley. At 6.30pm fetching suppers and washing up. Last three quarters of an hour spent working in the Nurses' dining room. At 8.30pm own supper and so to bed. Jobs in between, at any time, have included helping to set up 'Balkan Beams' from which broken legs are strung to keep them straight while mending, taking and fetching patients from theatres, x-ray and ambulances. I have also shaved a patient who can't sit up, bathed a patient who was liable to faint, filled hot water bottles and oiled the stretcher-carriers. I have not yet been in the theatre during an operation, only as far as the anaesthetic room.

Our quarters are in a converted ward block with our own kitchen and dining come sitting room, where we can listen to the radio and read the papers. The sleeping cubicles are very narrow with thin walls, but o.k. My fellow conchies are quite an idealistic lot but very easy to get on with – some would like to be in the FAU but have commitments and need to earn a small wage *[our earnings went direct to the FAU HQ]*. The organisation was set up at the start of the war, some have been at Spiceland *[Friends Relief Service training establishment, Devon]*, although having nothing to do with the Society of Friends. The Section leader is Stuart Walters, only 22 but has a BA in Botany.

As I think I said the country around here is very fine, not as grand as the Lakes but the Mendips have a beauty of their own, with a view across the Bristol Channel into South Wales. I have been thinking quite a bit recently about my religious position and in particular why I never pray formally. On my last free afternoon I went up into the hills and with all that splendid view and quietness around me, I began to ponder. And it came to me quite suddenly that I don't pray formally, because I don't feel it is right or profitable to demand that God rearrange the universe for me. I realised that I knew God to the extent that I knew myself at that moment. There is only one value, one reality, life. I must try to be great enough in spirit to help others show love to the whole world, like those who have shown me love. I also recalled what Mr Harris had often told us that we must think for ourselves and not be warped to the purposes of leaders who would make us hate each other blindly, and to try to develop a soul unswayed by the shouts of the crowd, to keep our ideals quietly and hand them on to others in the spirit of St Christopher. This is where I am at the moment, but I hope it doesn't sound too naïve and smug!

The story of this group can be found in a small booklet, The Winford Team: a record of the life and work of a group of conscientious objectors engaged on orderly duties at Winford Hospital, Bristol, 1940–1944 *by Tim Evens and Stuart Walters, 1945. Following my time at Winford Hospital, I returned home for a few days before travelling to Birmingham to join the Friends Ambulance Unit early in September.*

18th FAU Training Camp, Manor Farm, Northfield, Birmingham, 10 October 1943

Life continues its hectic pace here. We have lectures every day, First Aid with Dr *[Hubert]* Rutter, Nursing with Sister Gibbs, Fire Fighting by members of the BWFB *[British Women's Fire Brigade]*, Light Rescue by BARP *[British Air Raid Precautions]*, Poisonous gases by an FAU officer, and so on. We have also had some very interesting talks – Horace Alexander on Quakerism, he is coming again to talk on India, Jack Hoyland on India, Selby Clewer on China and the Unit, also Tegla Davies on the FAU constitution, Sandy Parnis on FAU finance, and Ian Nicholson on FAU work in hospitals. As I think I have said there is a Camp Commandant, a Training Officer, Medical Officer and a Catering Officer, but we really have not been too lucky with our Training Officers, what a job anyway! The first, Stanley Hancock, had to leave as both his parents were killed in an accident, the second, Bill Spray, was called away to lead a medical unit which will be attached to the Free French Forces, and now we have David Tod, a rather solemn character. Bill Spray was a very tough on us, but very popular. On his last day as the morning run was finishing, some rather enthusiastic types jumped on him, stripped him and dumped him in a full horse trough, just to show there was no ill feeling. What a parting gift – it was that nice frosty morning last week!

One day a week each section is on orderly duty. I was put in charge of the cooking, with seven helpers, although the Catering Officer kept an eye on things. We prepared meals for 60, with only paper instructions. We made porridge, cheese cakes, roast beef, rice pudding and jam tarts, without any major mishaps. Quite fun really, but I wouldn't want to do it every day, even with helpers to peel the spuds and wash up.

On the social front I had a phone call from Celia Newton *[Reg's girl-friend, she was also at St Christopher]* inviting me over for tea, as Reg would be there for the weekend *[she lived with her mother who had a general practice in Birmingham]*. Unfortunately, I was on duty so had to say no, but she

The lake at Manor Farm, round which the FAU trainees had to run each morning before breakfast. The grounds are now a public park. (Photo Jack Skeel, from FAU collection, Friends House Library)

hopes to arrange another time. Alison *[Cooper, a friend from school]* wrote to say that a bomb was dropped on Jordans a few days ago. There are a number of aircraft guns in the area, which they think were the target, and I always thought Jordans was such a quiet place!

The other day we had a formal discussion on the Christian purpose of the Unit. Christian principles underlie all of camp life. Every evening there is a 'devotional', which is really a shortened meeting for worship, only about 20 mins., not compulsory, of course, but always well attended, and there is also a brief reading at breakfast. In the discussion some felt that the Unit existed simply to get needy jobs done, others felt that relief and medical work had to be undertaken in a spirit of love, and that as a Christian pacifist group, which experienced such fellowship and companionship itself, it had an important witness to make…

18 FAU Training Camp, Manor Farm, Northfield, Birmingham, 17 October 1943

It never seems to stop raining here and everywhere is so wet. We had our first all day manoeuvre last week on the Lickey Hills, a bit like Sherrards Wood *[near Welwyn Garden City]*, but with open heathland in places, and about 600ft up, covering a considerable area. We had to search and find imaginary wounded cases and take them back to an ADS *[Advanced Dressing Station]* for treatment. The stretchers, with a live body on board, had to be negotiated over a 6ft wall, through a knee deep river, and when one finally arrived at the ADS we were sent out to find further casualties. Fortunately I was 'wounded' on the way back and taken to a Casualty Clearing Station and spent the rest of the time drinking tea and being treated for bullet wounds. A few days later we had a 'commando' course in the fields by the camp, modelled on an Royal Army Medical

Left: Manor Farm, Northfield (photo: Jack Skeel). Right: Dr Rutter at Manor Farm, during a previous training camp. (FAU collection, Friends House Library)

Corps course. It involved treating the 'patient', bandaging and putting on splints etc., getting him on a stretcher and again carrying it over various obstacles – fences, ditches, steep banks, hedges, a stream and even a small waterfall...

We've also had a variety of inoculations. I feel o.k. apart from a stiff arm, and we have also had our blood classified. I'm universal O...

Last Friday we had a camp concert when a group of young women, the Arden Singers, entertained us with a variety of songs, and we enjoyed a meal with them afterwards. On Sunday I went to meeting for worship at Northfield Meeting, a nice modern meeting house, there are two others quite near here – Bournville and Selly Oak – but I haven't been to either yet. On Sunday a small group of us had a scrumptious tea with the Cadbury family and a bath in their palatial bathroom. There are no facilities for bathing in camp, but it has been arranged that we all have a weekly bath at Dame Cadbury's 'palace', which really is a huge mansion on the other side of the estate, and even boasts a lift to the upper floors – all built I suppose on profits from cocoa!

Reg *[Middleton]* came over last Saturday, he is now working at Barnsley Hall Hospital at Bromsgrove, and I cycled back with him to see the FAU section there, and also Pam *[Burgess, another St Christopher old scholar]* who is at the Occupational Therapy school there. Reg will be leaving soon to go on a driving and vehicle maintenance course at Failands, near Bristol...

We had an 18 mile route march on Tuesday night, woken up at 12.30 pm and started marching at 1am. By 4am we were at Barnsley Hall where the FAU Section gave us hot cocoa, but after a 40 min rest we were off again, not arriving back at camp till 7.30am. When marching through a suburb a number of women on their way to work , shouted at us 'go

18th Friends Ambulance Unit training camp, September–November 1943 at Manor Farm.
Clifford in front row, second from left. Others later in 2 FAU Relief Team in Europe: David Curtis back row ninth from left,
Roger Stanger second row eleventh from left, and Gordon Taylor second from right.

down the mines you bloody conchies!'. The march leader stopped off to talk to them and explain we weren't out enjoying ourselves, but were in the process of training to look after those wounded by war. After breakfast we were allowed to sleep till 12am. Next week we have a longer march. I suppose it enhances our fitness somehow...

Clifford at Manor Farm

One afternoon we had a talk by Professor Kenneth Mellanby on malaria, during which he asked for volunteers to help him on his trials. I thought this was something I could do but thought I had better tell you about it first... Owing to the war in the Far East the Japanese have gained control of 90% of the world's supplies of quinine, which has led to a severe shortage elsewhere. A new drug Mepacrin or Atebrin is now being used as a treatment on those who have already been afflicted with the disease, but Mellanby believes it can and should be used as a prophylactic, hence the experimental trials. At present he is using some 25 FAU lads in London as 'guinea pigs'. They were all given differing dosages of the drug on a daily basis and then bitten by mosquitoes carrying malaria, some of the mosquitoes were 'clean', for control purposes. Blood tests are made every week, although everyone has acquired a yellow jaundiced appearance, no malaria parasites have been found in anyone's blood, so it seems to work. Mellanby now wants to try it on the Italian breed of mosquito, which carry the malaria plasmodium of the Southern European type, and is going to that part of Italy occupied by the Allies to fetch some mosquitoes. He will dissect and remove the plasmodium and put it in some of his own 'clean' mosquitoes. To 'clean' them the mosquitoes are flown at over 20,000 ft, which rids them of any other disease apparently. We would start the experiments when we arrive at our London training hospital after camp is over. Well, I have already volunteered, but I thought I had better tell you in case you have some very real objection, but I bet Daddy will be interested and wish he had the opportunity to take part! *[My father was the librarian at the London School of Hygiene and Tropical Medicine.]* Unfortunately, I have developed some sort of Tinea in the groin, it is really rather sore, and the MO has taken me off all exercises. Dr Rutter is giving me some treatment.

As camp is to finish soon it has been suggested that on my way home

I should call in and see the MO *[Medical Officer]* at FAU HQ in Gordon Square, if it is no better... As I write this I am listening to some fine piano playing by an FAU chap. He is only 19, but has already composed some of his own music, which he refuses to allow to be published yet. I am sure it will be one day as he obviously has a future. He is known as Julian.

I noticed an obituary for Julian Budden in The Guardian *on 7 March 2007, where he was described as an opera scholar, radio producer and broadcaster. He graduated in Classics at Oxford before studying at the Royal College of Music and obtaining a BMus at the Trinity College of Music. He worked at the BBC for 32 years, where he started by supplying notes for music announcers, finally progressing to Chief Producer of opera. He wrote articles for* The Listener *and several books, his chief legacy being a three volume work on the Verdi operas and a biography of the composer. He retired early to go and live with Luigi Innocenti, a potter, but continued to write on music. He received many awards and prizes. So I was right, he did have a future.*

When Camp ended in November, I had a few days at home while the Tinea cleared up and then went to Lewisham Hospital in south London, where I had experience on both medical and surgical wards, outpatients and casualty departments, and at night firewatching on the hospital roof during air raids. The top floor wards had all been left empty, on the assumption that small bombs wouldn't penetrate any further, but the ward facilities enabled hot drinks to be made there so that firewatchers could warm up from time to time throughout the night. Later the hospital was hit by a bomb, shortly after I had left, which killed a nurse I had known and started a fierce fire. The FAU Section Leader, Alan Taylor, at considerable risk, managed to retrieve a number of gas cylinders which were about to explode from the heat. He was awarded an MBE for his courage. After the war he qualified as doctor.

Lewisham Hospital, London SE13, 9 November 1943

Lewisham is I understand a typical London County Council hospital, very large with some 30 wards, modern in some parts very Victorian in others... We have had an air raid for several nights running, mostly uneventful for us, although two nights ago while I was on fire watching duty, we heard two bombers overhead, the ack-ack guns set up a terrific racket, and shrapnel started to shower down all over the place. I was very glad of my tin hat! Later one of the FAU who had been working in Casualty said 10 cases had been brought in, two of whom had died, both railwaymen, from phosphorus burns...

Lewisham Hospital, London SE13, 18 November 1943

Work on the ward is much the same, but I have been to theatre on three occasions now. I simply stand at the back and watch, but it is useful experience – pretty routine ops. I gather, appendectomy, colostomy and the resetting of a broken jaw. Every three weeks I change jobs, different wards, and outpatients, where I have given my first injections… We haven't started on the malaria trials yet, although we have had our blood tested. I'm told I have very healthy blood, haemoglobin 112%, the average is around 90%...

It was so nice to see Daddy and Uncle Eric the other day, pity it couldn't have been for longer…

There are seven of us in the section, and sometimes we can get time off together. We have a 'devotional' some evenings, and on others we have a German lesson among ourselves. We are learning from *Heute Abend*, but the 'Square' *[FAU HQ]* only sent us four copies for the seven of us, so we have to share. Does Freda still use her copy?... Yes, I do have a pair of woollen gloves for firewatching, they have a few holes but still do the job… I will try to come home on my day off during Christmas week, but the fare will be 4s 6d, I couldn't afford coming more than once…

Lewisham Hospital, London SE13, 30 November 1943

I've changed wards yet again, I suppose it's all good experience. We started the malaria trials two weeks ago with increasing doses of mepacrin and have now been bitten eight times from mosquitoes carrying Benign Tertiary Malaria. I am starting to turn a bit yellow, and am due to be bitten again next Friday. So far the blood withdrawn tested negative for malaria parasites and adequate for the quantity of Atebrin (Mepacrin).

Yesterday I finished work with a temperature of a 101.8°, so I went to bed, took an asprin and a dose of Atebrin, and in the morning it was down to 99°. But on the Section Leader's orders I stayed in bed but got up this afternoon, so I was able to write this letter. I am feeling rather tired, but don't have a cold. However, I can hardly think it is due to the malaria, the incubation period is not long enough…

There was a three month gap following this letter, but as far as I can remember I went down with a chest infection soon after, and had several days in bed on the ward I had been working on and was then sent home to convalesce. Which may account partly for the gap, or maybe my parents simply failed to keep some letters. When I recovered I returned to Lewisham for a time and was then sent to Barnsley Hall Hospital in Bromsgrove, from where the next letter came.

2. Worcestershire and West Lothian

March to December 1944

Barnsley Hall EMS Hospital, Bromsgrove, Worcs.,
12 March 1944
Despite having to change trains at Rugby the journey was not too bad. The Section Leader is away at present, so for the time being I am working with Reg on one of the theatres. It is quite a relaxed regime here – 9.00am to 6.00pm, with 1½ hours for lunch, and Saturday afternoon and Sunday off, although one is on call all the time for emergencies…

Barnsley Hall EMS Hospital, Bromsgrove, Worcs.,
15 March 1944
When the Section Leader, Bert Jones returned, he took me off the theatre and put me on a chest ward, most of the patients have TB. The work is not hard but rather unpleasant, emptying and measuring the contents of sputum mugs and the like… the rest of the day I do general portering around the hospital…

Barnsley Hall EMS Hospital, Bromsgrove, Worcs.,
16 April 1944
After a couple of weeks I was taken off the ward and returned to the theatre as Reg has left and is now stationed in London. The theatre is very busy, operations going on most of the day. Working hours are determined by the 'ops', and sometimes run late into the evening. There are two American Army surgeons who do some of the ops. One of the woman anaesthetists is married to an FAU man who is abroad at the moment… Have a nice holiday in the Cotswolds, Cinderford is near the Severn, isn't it?

Barnsley Hall EMS Hospital, Bromsgrove, Worcs., 23 April 1944

I'm still on theatre and enjoying the experience. Work starts at 9.00am with sorting out dirty laundry and scrubbing out bins. Then drums are loaded with gowns, caps, masks, towels, etc. for sterilising in the Auto-clave. I am responsible for this, a job that lasts off and on all day, load after load, one hour for each load. In between I clean and prepare the anaesthetic trolleys and stay on hand to help the anaesthetist during ops. in case a gas cylinder needs changing or any other odd job. On Satur-day mornings the theatre and tables and stools are scrubbed and all the instruments checked and cleaned before sterilising... I have been offered a place on a driving and vehicle maintenance course at Clent in about two weeks, I have accepted, although I would have preferred to go to Failand, which is a longer and more technical course.

FAU, Moor Hall Farm, Clent, Nr Stourbridge, Worcs., 14 May 1944

Well I arrived here on the 7th May and am happily installed. The Clent hills rise to about 800ft with some fine views of the Vale of Severn, the Malverns and Clee Hill. This is a lovely farmhouse we are living in, a little small for all of us, but the food is great. We have one of the trained Unit cooks, and as we are near the FAU Midland Assembly Depot where food is stored we tend to get above the ration. The farm is owned by Cadbury's and supplies milk for the chocolate factory. I'm really enjoy-ing things. In the mornings we do a bit of necessary house work and then go to the workshops – dismantling car engines, etc. Afternoons we have driving lessons and do car maintenance and servicing. In the eve-nings we have lectures and films. I never thought I should so enjoy shov-ing my head into oily engines, and tinkering under lorries. I now have 7 hours of driving behind me and seem to be progressing, although I have given the instructors a few hairy moments, but I now roll along at a steady 30mph without undue worry. The emphasis is on lorry driving which includes learning to double de-clutch on crash gear boxes. There is a variety of vehicles – a 2½ ton Morris truck, a 30cwt Commer truck, two Austin sevens, a Morris car and a Wolseley. There is a Vauxhall for practising servicing on only, and two lorries that can no longer be driven. In the workshop there are three car engines for dismantling and reas-sembling, an MG 8 cylinder, a Citroen and a Bedford. We have lessons in car mechanics and electrics.

*An FAU mechanics' course similar to Clifford's but held at Manor Farm
(Photograph: Jack Skeel, FAU collection, Friends House Library)*

You mention leave, it would look as though I would be due for some at the end of this course. It begins to look as though the Allies are planning something big. Reg *[Middleton]* has joined the 12th Field Surgical Unit, which had been in the Middle-East but was recalled to be re-equipped ready for the next phase, they are stationed in some RAMC barracks...

FAU, Moor Hall Farm, Clent, Nr Stourbridge, Worcs., 28 May 1944

I'm having a splendid time here, although we work hard it is so absorbing, and it's great to be in the fresh air, and look up from car servicing to see the distant hills, or the gracefully sweeping valleys. It has been really warm recently and gets quite hot inside the cars despite the sunshine roofs. I have now driven in Kidderminster and Birmingham where the tramlines and traffic add a different dimension... Yesterday, John Pye and I went to Bewdley and took a rowing boat on the Severn, a very pleasant change... I have also climbed up in the Clent Hills, but everywhere was shrouded in mist that day. Gaydu *[from St Christopher School; see page 75]* is waiting for his commission and Reg is with his unit lying fully equipped in some southern port, waiting for what, I wonder? There are several FAU units who do very similar work to the RAMC, but under their own authority and the Army is happy to accept this. However their attitude to relief work is not so accommodating. It seems that

General Eisenhower, the American Commander in Chief, has no desire for voluntary bodies. In Italy, for instance, all the relief work reinforcements have been cancelled, and it is not certain whether the work can continue. The whole Unit is alive with talk about relief work in Europe and it is clear this is what most people want to do.

There is to be a major meeting at FAU HQ in Gordon Square to plan policy for the next year, it should be most interesting, I don't know yet if we are sending a representative.

FAU, Moor Hall Farm, Clent, Nr Stourbridge, Worcs., 11 June 1944

So it has come at last *[the Allied invasion of Europe had started on D-Day with the landings in France on the 6th of June]*. From all the welter of radio and newspaper reports, one thing has impressed me, they all seem so sober and realistic, with hardly any of the glorification one might have expected. One correspondent, Solon, in the *News Chronicle* described how French people had lived during the past few months and how some were even sorry for some of the German soldiers, who had often told them they didn't want to do what they were doing, and had mostly behaved in a polite and correct manner. I haven't heard anything like that before. It must be hopeful that people are reacting in such a realistic way, to what is a very momentous, history changing event. Here we are trying to come

Mechanics' course, Manor Farm

to terms with what it may mean for us, and although an opportunity, our witness may be that much harder. Will people's attitude to us conchies revert to how it was at the time of Dunkirk and the fall of France? The King has urged people to turn to prayer... Along with others I have been thinking about what it will mean for us. After the 9.00pm news on the wireless on Tuesday I sat and pondered, and some words of Wordsworth went through my mind –

If this great world of joy and pain
revolve in one sure track;
If freedom, set, will rise again,
And virtue, flown, come back;

Woe to the selfish crew who fill
The heart with each day's care
Nor gain, from past or future, skill
To bear, and to forbear!

Over the weekend Richard Wainwright *[after the war he became a Liberal Democrat MP and their party spokesman on financial matters]* came to discuss with us all individually our next step in the Unit. The possibilities of overseas work is still obscure, mainly because the authorities have yet to make clear their position on voluntary bodies doing relief work in

Mechanics' course, Manor Farm

Army occupied areas of Europe. For the time being he thought I would be transferred to a new section being established at a hospital that had been set aside for casualties from France and was very short of orderlies. I accepted this but asked if anything came up with driving involved I would like to be considered for that, and registered my long term interest in work overseas...On Saturday I was asked to drive a lorry into Birmingham to take one of the Camp officers on some bank business. As I had time to spare, I went into Hudson's, the large bookshop there, and quite by chance ran into two of the boys who had been at Winford. One had now joined the Unit and was at Lichfield Hospital and the other was working at the Queen Elizabeth Hospital in Birmingham. He said that on three successive nights they had convoys of nearly 100 casualties from the fighting in France, and could take no more. They were so overwhelmed that they had called on the help of the FAU at the MAD *[Midland Assembly Depot]* in the middle of the night! The FAU left some members behind to form a temporary section to run a ward for wounded German prisoners, which he said includes one or two Russians who had been fighting with the German Army... I asked Richard Wainwright, when he was here, if he had any news of the 12th FSU, you may remember this is the section Reg is with. He said they had every reason to believe they were now in France. The 12th FSU has quite a history, it was lead by Henry Headley and was with the Free French Army all the way from Egypt to Tunis. There was a report about them in the *Daily Mirror*, which described them as 'strange heroes', when they declined the award of the Africa Star... Gaydu wrote to tell me he is now having officer training at a pre-OCTU *[Officer Cadet Training Unit]*. Thank Freda for the info. about the old scholars reunion, but I shan't be making it this year.

> *The driving and vehicle maintenance course finished in mid-June and as expected I was transferred to Ronkswood Emergency Hospital in Worcester, which had been entirely cleared to deal with casualties following the D-Day landings and was struggling to cope. A new FAU section had been formed to help.*

Ronkswood Hospital, Worcester, 25 June 1944

Life here is as much as I expected. We sleep in a hut building some way away from the hospital and have to traipse over to the hospital for a bath. We are working here on an emergency basis, mainly for stretcher bearing when the convoys come in from the railway station. The orderlies are a mixture of conchies, paid civilians and some ex-soldiers who were invalided out for mental reasons (shell-shock, I suppose). Our meals are taken in another building with all the orderlies, RAMC personnel, soldiers who do guard duties and wardmasters... The hospital is modern and well equipped and the work not unpleasant, in between stretcher bearing I work on X-ray, mainly developing in the dark room. Our hours are 9.00 to 5.00, but the convoys always come in after dark *[not to alarm the civilian population at the large numbers?]* and getting them into bed or X-rayed for ops the following day can take well into the night. We have had three convoys so far with over a 50 patients on each occasion. It is rather depressing to see stretcher after stretcher going in with so many young men, some maybe maimed for life. Most interesting, though, is the reception given to two wounded German soldiers, who had to be put on the same ward as British casualties, there was little animosity and they cheerfully responded to being called 'Fritz'. They both said they hated Nazism, and said Germany had lost the war, but we had to be beware of the Russians. John Corsellis who speaks fluent German is working on the ward, and they were incredulous when he explained he was allowed to be a conscientious objector. More harrowing were the stories told by some British paratroopers, who were so glad to be back out of that 'hell', as they called it. They claimed that before being dropped they were given orders not to take any prisoners as being behind the lines there would be no means of coping with them till support troops arrived, which of course meant shooting them! So much for the Geneva Convention! There are so many other stories we have been told, but they will have to wait for another time, although I also found it interesting that in Bayeux the Allied troops were warmly cheered, but in some places people ran out to spit at them for bringing so much destruction to their villages. I haven't seen that in the papers...

Ronkswood Hospital, Worcester, 4 July 1944

It is extremely busy here and it doesn't show any signs of easing up. Even the Occupational Therapy block has been turned into wards. How can the papers say we are only suffering light casualties! We understand Barnsley Hall Hospital have said they can take no more. The theatre here has not stopped for 60 hours, with shifts of different surgeons and nurses. Very many cases have to be X-rayed before being operated on, and I never seem to get out of the dark room. We are getting many more German soldiers now and some Poles. John Corsellis, who speaks German, and works on the ward that has now been given over entirely to them, says there is one young boy who is very Nazi, and although badly wounded won't be treated and has refused a blood transfusion. John says his outlook is grim. One or two of the older German men have asked

John why he is not in the army and he has explained to them about the FAU and gave one of them, who reads a little English, a Quaker booklet. He later thanked him and said he was amazed that there were people who could think like that! The Poles were conscripted into units to fight the Allies, whether against their wishes or willingly, I don't know…Sorry to write all this war stuff, but we are living in very strange times at the moment.

Ronkswood Hospital, Worcester, 15 July 1944

In between times I am reading *Burma Surgeon*, really interesting, fascinating bits about the FAU team working with him *[Dr Seagrave, the author, was a missionary surgeon]*. Work goes on here relentlessly, although the convoys are now more spaced out which makes for more reasonable working hours. Large notices have gone up telling all staff it is a criminal offence to pass on any news or information given by the wounded soldiers about conditions or the fighting in France. So maybe I had better be more circumspect. Many of the soldiers who are getting better are beginning to realise they are probably out of it for good and are clearly more cheerful. Those who can get about are 'terrorising' the nurses. John Corsellis says the Nazi boy has now lost a leg, but fears it is too late for him and that he is dying. John goes to talk with him most evenings in his free time and he is at last showing some appreciation. John has written an article for the *FAU Chronicle* about his time with these wounded German soldiers…

There is considerable movement in the FAU now that the authorities have lifted the ban on travel. Tegla Davies has set off to visit FAU sections around the world, which had been postponed because of the hostilities. Two large parties are leaving the MAD soon – the 16th China party and the 2nd Middle East Relief party, and a first party for relief work in northern Europe is now being assembled, it is hoped they will leave in September. Can all this freeing up of space mean we are not far behind?

I had my first letter from Reg last week since he arrived in France. I thought you might like to read this extract – 'Well here is the result of the invasion. We are in France! I expect you have seen in Weekly Information that we got over here. The trip across was longer than usual, and being one of those small landing craft, it rolled quite a bit, and the first day out I felt shocking and spent most of the time over the rail! I decided then and there never to go on any sea trips for pleasure. However, after the initial sea-sickness I was more or less alright. We lay all day on the deck on stretchers, and also had to sleep there as the bunks below were all taken. Actually it turned out we had the better place, as it was unbearably hot and stuffy below. We were fine on deck on our stretchers with a couple of blankets and a sleeping bag. The wind was blowing quite hard and occasionally we were covered in sea spray, when the bows went down. I slept well, felt terrific on waking and tucked in to tinned turkey and peaches. After disembarking and getting organised we had an hour or so to spare and walked into a village nearby. We saw an oldish man unloading wood so we gave him a hand and he invited us in for a cup of tea. It turned out he had been keeping the tea for five years during the German occupation for just such an occasion! For obvious reasons I can't say much about what we are doing or where we are, sorry about that, as I expect you are itching to know what its like for when you come over. All I can say is that things aren't what I had expected.'

Gaydu wrote to say he is still training to be an officer, and I was so glad to know Owen is back again. Is it the third or fourth time he has been sunk? *[Owen Fountain, a boyhood friend, was a radio operator in the merchant navy.]*

On my free afternoon I went into Worcester, it was lovely and sunny and I walked through Kings College green with the cathedral on one side and the college on the other scattered with willow trees. Further on I passed terraces with lawns and little stoned grey walls, down to the river. It is surprisingly wide at this point with grassy banks where I saw some college boys launching their rowing boats. Across the river one can see the Malverns in the distance. I came across what I guessed was the Kings College cricket ground and I watched the boys in their whites and heard the tonk of the ball as it met the well oiled willow of the bat. Very English I felt and I couldn't help comparing it to a game of American Army baseball I had seen earlier played in Worcester in aid of the Red Cross. Where they were all dressed in bright yellow and blue clothes with some very ugly peaked caps on their heads *[little did I know how ubiquitous they were to become]*, while a military band played loud music. Obviously many people were attracted to it, but I know which I prefer!

Ronkswood Hospital, Worcester, 30 July 1944

...only two convoys so far this week... quite a few tankmen with severe facial and hand burns, from being trapped in their tanks, I guess. Reg said his unit had been visited by General 'Monty' and 20 cigs to all and sundry were handed out... he said they are having amazing success with Penicillin, what a miracle drug for treating infected wounds...

I desperately need some new clothes, my old green jacket is worn right through at the elbows, and my pair of grey trousers, well they just aren't! Maybe it will not be much longer before I get a khaki uniform.

Ronkswood Hospital, Worcester 4 August 1944

Last Tuesday we had a convoy at 2am! Ron Tansley our section leader has been moved to the heavy driving section at Leominster. The new leader has transferred me to theatre work as I have the experience – they are frightfully busy, sometimes with 4 tables going at once, which is a bit hair-raising. I gather the 'Buzz' bombs in London are really bad at the moment and Lewisham Hospital has been hit again…

Ronkswood Hospital, Worcester, 10 August 1944

My leave has been cancelled, but only temporarily, I hope. We had a telegram from HQ yesterday putting all the Section except Michael and myself on embarkation leave, in preparation for a little trip to France. We are to stay here for a short time as we are both on theatre, and so let the hospital down more gently in this area. It looks as though they will close the Section soonish…

Ronkswood Hospital, Worcester, 15 August 1944

Sorry I haven't written sooner to explain about the leave, but we had two convoys over the weekend, which involved me working from 4am to 6pm with only a break for meals, and yesterday from 8am to 10. 30pm. No sooner is the stretcher bearing finished than it's into the theatre, but today it was over by 7pm, so I had time to write… Apart from Michael and myself all the Section have left on embarkation leave and we are only here till 26 August.

I will come home for some leave and Michael *[surname unknown]* will go to another section. It was a pity I couldn't join you at Almeley, I would have loved to have seen the Black Mountains again. When I look west from here I only see the Malverns, mind you they look beautiful in the setting sun, all purplish colours…

With the closure of the Section at Ronkswood Hospital, I took some leave that was owing and was then posted back to Barnsley Hall where the Unit had been depleted by members being sent overseas.

Barnsley Hall EMS Hospital, Bromsgrove, Worcs., 17 September 1944

The journey up was quick only stopping at Coventry and Birmingham, although I had to stand in the corridor, but that's par for the course. I bumped in to Michael Tutt at King's Cross *[another Chris old scholar]*. He is in the Navy and was on his way to Northern Ireland so we walked together to Euston station. He's been having an exciting time on MTBs *[motor torpedo boats]* in the English Channel. Barnsley Hall is much the same but the Section is considerably smaller and all seems quieter than I remember it, there hasn't been a convoy for over two weeks. I've been on Centre Theatre and then on Plaster Theatre, but I asked for a change and I am now working in the stores – issuing new supplies, etc.

Barnsley Hall Hospital, Bromsgrove, Worcs., 1 October 1944

After a longish lull convoys are coming in again. Yesterday we had some 50 stretcher cases around 7pm and then in the night about 4am 80 walking cases, it turned out they had come straight from the battle at Arnhem. Tired and dirty, even torn tunics with the mud of Holland on their boots. It must have been a real hell! There were a number who were not actually injured but sent for a check up as they were suffering from exposure and exhaustion. Very tired looking faces and staring eyes, although with a sort of undaunted grin on their unshaven faces, 'England at last' they said...

Reg has written from Belgium and has been very busy, he just longs for a bath and a bed with clean sheets, army blankets are so itchy... I cycled over to Northfield the other evening where the 20th Camp was holding a 'send off' occasion for the Yugoslavia Hospital group who are going to Italy. I met two old Lewisham boys, who had been back to the hospital and they told me the Unit living quarters had been demolished in the bombing, and the Section now had to live in the Nurses Home. One of the nurses I knew on the Outpatients department had been killed...

Barnsley Hall Hospital, Bromsgrove, Worcs., 15 October 1944

One of the Section, Gordon *[Taylor]*, who worked on Theatre Two has left to take up a driving job in London, so I have had to take his position. I'm a bit fed up as I dislike the stuffy atmosphere and would far rather be out of doors, never mind. I wrote to HQ asking if they had a driving job, and I had a nice reply saying they would see what could done... I had a letter from 'Smithy' *[Peter Quinton Smith, a St Christopher old scholar]*. He was wounded on a Normandy beach in June and is still in hospital, but sounded quite cheerful. He had a wound in his thigh big enough to put a fist into, the nerves were damaged and his foot dropped, and he has to wear a boot with a spring attachment... I had a small parcel from Auntie Con with a hundred fags! Most unexpected, but very much appreciated.

Barnsley Hall Hospital, Bromsgrove, Worcs., 21 October 1944

In great haste. I had word from HQ that they have a job for me at Bangour Hospital, half driving – half ward work. So I have to pack up in a hurry as I am off to Scotland tonight!

I moved to Scotland from where the next letter came.

The Farmhouse, Bangour Hospital, Broxburn, West Lothian, 29 October 1944

I'm sorry I havn't written before but it's taken quite a time to settle in. My first impressions are good, apart from the cold, there is even a bit of snow on the tops of the hills behind the hospital. The hospital is situated off the main road between Glasgow and Edinburgh, which runs through an area littered with coal mines and oil shale wells. The country to the north, however, is splendid, one can see the hills shrouded in a blue mist, and large belts of fir trees and the occasional reservoir. I and another member of the team went for what we intended would be a short walk, but it was so enjoyable, over heathland with a red sky, and green and autumn tints, and it was only the growing darkness and the cold wind that eventually turned us for home.

The hospital is, I understand, a very large one with 3,000 beds, twenty theatres and four X-ray departments. The wards are all separate buildings spread over a vast area. The old hospital is known as 'Bangour village' and has a working farm adjacent to it. Several wards are for TB patients, both chest and orthopaedic, and two of the wards have only German casualties. There is also a mental hospital somewhere. There are ten of us in the FAU section and we are housed in a very spacious farmhouse with room for double that number, but we make up with innumerable cats and kittens all over the place. Three dailies come in to cook and do the chores for us. All very Scottish, as is the food too, porridge for breakfast, broth before dinner and supper without exception, but it's good and plentiful. We have a large open fire on which we burn logs, and I find I need six blankets on my bed at night! There are two Scotsmen on the team, who have to act as interpreters. One of the dailies saw me spill some milk on the floor and remarked 'dinna slitter the flair', which I had to think about.

My work is partly on a ward, interspersed with driving jobs as necessary, a Humber ambulance and Hillman car. Once a week I take patients to a convalescent home about seven miles away and bring others back, which makes for a nice run out. Because of the distances around the hospital food and other supplies have to be transported by the ambulance, and there are always patients to be ferried to X-ray and theatre. With the car there are rounds to make with the Matron or Night Sister, a job I share with the Section Leader. I work on a surgical TB ward – patients with TB in the spine or joints which is always a long term business sometimes taking years to clear up *[obviously before the drugs we have nowadays]*. Some are quite young boys and have to lie virtually motionless on their backs or fronts in plaster shells and have to be washed after they have used a bed pan. I'm so sorry for them and amazed at how cheerful they are. The nurses keep a jolly atmosphere going and even give of their free time in the evenings to come in and read stories to the young ones, and I have joined them to play draughts and so on. The older men also love to talk, and everyone has a laugh when I have difficulty with the accent.

I had a rather unpleasant experience on Thursday night. Following an emergency call I and the Section Leader went to the hospital centre to find that a Red Cross ambulance was already available, so with a doctor and two RAMC men we all went to an accident some way up the main road. A small car must have been travelling too fast, skidded and overturned, and two soldiers were badly injured and two sailors less so. We left the ambulance at the side of the road, to attend the injured, when a Polish Army vehicle failing to see the man waving a torch to slow the traffic down, crashed into the ambulance, and I saw one occupant shoot straight through the front windowscreen *[vehicles in wartime did not have proper headlights, only thin slits]*. Amazingly neither were badly injured, only bruises and slight cuts from the glass. I had to go into the road and flag down a car and hitch a lift back to the hospital so I could pick up our FAU ambulance, as the Red Cross ambulance was now immovable. Eventually we got all the injured to hospital with our ambulance, but one of the soldiers died during the night. It was all a bit of a shock, and it was the first time I had driven the ambulance at night, however I seem to have measured up alright. We had to make statements to the police as witnesses.

Interested to know that Michael Frankton *[a Welwyn boy]* is expecting to go to China. I have heard that no more FAU convoys are being sent there, but maybe he is an individual replacement for someone coming home... I expect to be here for some time, but Ian Nicholson is visiting the section on Nov 2 to discuss future plans, so I may learn something then. I can't see the fighting in Germany ending soon, and anyway once it is over there will be so much rehabilitation to do...

Bangour Hospital, Broxburn, West Lothian, Scotland
5 November 1944

We had quite a storm one night last week with ferocious winds and driving rain, trees were uprooted and chimney pots knocked off, but the locals assured us it was a seasonal occurrence. The wind and the rain came in from the north-west, howling up the valleys till it reached the Pentlands when it carried on sideways causing snow drifts several inches thick, but it melted away surprisingly quickly. Apparently in the spring it can get worse. Last year they had drifts several feet thick against the garage doors and the ambulance had to be dug out. We keep a lamp burning in the engine to prevent it freezing up in case we have an emergency. I have to say I find it all rather splendid, when the hills take on a menacing aspect as the dark black clouds come over almost touching the tops, with an uncanny bright light below. The weather has really been too bad for walking, but last Saturday I got a lift by ambulance into Edinburgh. It rained all afternoon, but I walked up Princes Street visited the Castle, looking over the battlements, the war memorial and St Mary's Chapel. By then I was so wet I found a nice café where I could dry out and had some tea and hot buttered toast. Then I queued for about half an hour and managed to get a seat to see *The Mikado* with the D'Oyly Carte who are just finishing a season here. I enjoyed it but only just managed to catch the last bus back. The hospital has two badminton courts in a covered building and I have been having some games recently... As expected Ian Nicholson visited the Section last Thursday and talked with each of us. As a result five members will be leaving soon to prepare for overseas work. He has arranged with the Section Leader for me to have a medical examination, and if fit he thought I would almost certainly be in the next large party going into Europe probably in the spring, which all sounds very hopeful... I enclose my 'sweet' coupons as I never seem able to spend them and I expect you can make do with them.

Bangour Hospital, Broxburn, West Lothian, Scotland,
12 November 1944

Very many thanks for the bumper parcel. The leather jacket looks great it will come in very handy. I meant you to use the sweet coupons for yourselves, but the choc will be very acceptable! The big news is that I have had a letter from HQ, I quote 'The Unit has been asked to prepare at very short notice sections amounting to 55 members for work in North-West Europe similar to that already undertaken by Gerald Gardiner's two teams. MAD *[Midland Assembly Depot]* can supply 33, and it is felt that this is sufficient for the time being, but we would like to have the remainder ready should they be needed. The primary need is for transport and emergency relief work for civilians in recently liberated areas. The request for these teams will probably come through the Red Cross and COBSRA *[Council of British Societies for Relief Abroad]* who may wish to ask the help of other voluntary bodies, so it is impossible to say exactly how many Unit members will be required. I know that you are interested in this type of work and have you in mind for one of these teams should we be asked to supply the whole 55. I would like to know if you would accept such an invitation. If it does come off, notice will be very short, and it would probably mean leaving your present work with very little warning. So could you please let me have your answer by return?'

The Section Leader has arranged for a medical examination for me and has had my inoculations checked up. I haven't had a diphtheria injection so are having the first one in a day or two...

Bangour Hospital, Broxburn, West Lothian, Scotland, 17 November 1944

A very brief note. I got a telegram at 8.00pm this evening asking me to report to MAD at Selly Wood by Saturday at the latest. In anticipation of being equipped there I am sending a lot of my stuff home now, and need to start packing. I imagine I will get some embarkation leave, but I will write again when I know more. I shall have to catch the night train to Birmingham tomorrow. It's all action stations now.

FAU, Midland Assembly Depot, Oak Tree Lane, Birmingham, 3 December 1944

Sorry I haven't written before but it's been all go here. Getting our uniforms, sewing our names on to what equipment we have got so far. Last rounds of injections and so on. We haven't received our transport yet – each team will have two Austin ambulances and two 30 cwt Ford trucks. Not a lot is known yet but we are to be given Second Lieutenant status which has officer privileges, so have had some amusing talks on security, officer behaviour, and the privilege of censoring one's own letters. You can send me letters, papers and parcels, but no food of any sort, and no money unless arranged through HQ...

After being fully equipped most members were sent on embarkation leave, so I had a few days at home.

46

FAU, Midland Assembly Depot, Oak Tree Lane, Birmingham, 24 December 1944

I missed the train coming back, but I was in good company as I met up with eight others. We caught a later train, but only had the mildest of reprimands for being late. We found a feverish state of excitement as news was expected at any time. Sure enough, we shortly had a 48 hour notice of movement and promptly set about packing everything up. Then at the very last moment it was cancelled. Apparently all the shipping was requisitioned to carry over reinforcements to cover for the troops who had been moved to counter Runstedt's offensive in the Ardennes. In view of this delay, Gerald tried to discover from the War Office if he could send us all home for Christmas, however, this was not granted as convoys were being made up all the time and we still might be asked to move at any time. So we shall have to make do here.

It's all a bit frustrating as we are just hanging about. Through the window I can see the lines of our trucks and ambulances standing in the Birmingham drizzle waiting to take us on the next stage of our adventure.

In the event the teams had their Christmas dinner on Christmas Eve and the convoy, over 20 vehicles, travelled down to the south coast on Christmas Day on very icy roads.

Transit Camp, somewhere in England [Tilbury Docks], 28 December 1944

We are still here but expecting to get our movement order at any moment. I do hope you had a good Christmas at Uncle Stanley's. We had our Christmas dinner on Christmas Eve and the convoy travelled down on Christmas Day, it took us all day, we could only drive slowly as the roads were icy in places. This is a vast place with hundreds of Nissen huts. I can't tell you very much, but it's a bit primitive although the food is good, and there has been some really ropy variety entertainment put on in the evenings. Well there isn't much to say except that I'm fine, only wanting to get on with things. This will probably be my last letter this side of the water...

3. Ostend to the Rhine and the Weser

January to April 1945

The FAU teams with their ambulances and trucks duly sailed out of Tilbury at the end of the year aboard an LST (Landing Ship Tank). I remember it was a journey that took far longer than had been anticipated, with heavy weather, and at one time the seamen had to ask for our help in going round tightening the chains which held some of the vehicles to the deck, which we had to do in between bouts of sea-sickness over the rails. It was prolonged as the sea was too rough for the ships to enter the port of Ostend, only recently liberated, with the debris from the demolition and other obstructions left in the harbour by the departing German Army not yet cleared. So the ships had to stay out at sea for several hours while the weather calmed sufficiently for them to make a safer entrance. As there was a fear of attack from U-boats the vessels had to keep on the move by sailing in wide circles.

FAU, 205 Det. CA [Civil Affairs], Rear HQ 30 Corps, BLA [British Liberation Army; Antwerp], 1 January 1945
Well here I am safe and sound. If you have had my letter from the transit camp you must have been waiting for this one. The crossing was longer than usual and rather rough. I was pretty sick, and so were most of the others, but we soon got over it once we had our feet on firm land, and found we wanted to have hot drinks and eat! There is much I would like to tell you but I fear censorship prevents... When a convoy of vehicles passes through the little villages, everyone seems to come out to cheer, even small babies wrapped in furs waving tiny woollen gloved hands. If we stop by the roadside children swarm around, jabbering away, which we do our best to understand. They have taken all my English pennies as souvenirs... We are now settled in a large town *[Antwerp]* but are already making preparations to move to our first real job soon. A balaclava hat wouldn't be out of place here, and another pair of woolly gloves. Granmervie's *[grandmother's]* socks are great!

FRIENDS' AMBULANCE UNIT

Telephone:
MUSeum 5986   **5th.** January 1945   4, Gordon Square, LONDON W.C.1.

PRIVATE - INFORMATION CONTAINED IN THIS LETTER MUST
NOT BE GIVEN TO THE PRESS WITHOUT REFERENCE TO THIS
OFFICE

North West Europe Party No.2

Dear Friend,

    This party has now reached the Continent and letters and parcels should for the moment be addressed to our H.Q. in the North West who will forward them.

        Name,
        F.A.U.,
        Att. B.C.R.S. Civilian Relief,
        B.R.C. Commission,
        H.Q.1,
        B.L.A.

  Postage Rates:
        Letters 1½d.
        Parcels 9d. for three pounds
        1/6d. for seven pounds

    We expect that as members take up work as teams in different areas they will use separate addresses of which they will no doubt notify you.

Coupons for Knitting We are able to supply coupons for wool to parents or dependents of members, who may wish to knit garments for them. An estimate of the amount of wool required must be sent to us and we will then send you the required number of coupons, at the rate of one coupons for two ozs of wool. The finished articles must be returned to this office together with any unused wool - unless this be used towards another article for which additional coupons are requested at the same time. We undertake to despatch the parcel.

                Yours sincerely,

                Ronald Joynes

            Overseas Officer

Letter sent by the FAU headquarters to Clifford's parents

The FAU party was split into five Sections, of ten or twelve men each; three teams staying in Antwerp, and two moving to more forward areas. Other members were sent to join the two original teams, who had landed in France in September and were now working in other parts of Belgium. I was in this group. The teams in Antwerp were involved in civilian defence helping the local ambulance and hospital services, as the town and port were under day and night aerial attack. As a measure of the intensity, it is of interest to note that while 1,050 V-2 rocket bombs landed in the London area killing over 2,500 Britons, some 30,000 people were killed in Antwerp from these weapons. In one terrible instance a cinema was hit and very many, including allied soldiers, were killed.

FAU, 205 Det. CA, Rear HQ 30 Corps, BLA [Antwerp], 3 January 1945

I'm still where I was when I last wrote, and have had plenty of time to explore the town, which swarms with allied forces. Some damage, but people very cheerful and seem genuinely pleased at the allies' presence here. At first appearances the shops seem well stocked, even more than at home, but this is an illusion as it is only luxury items, watches, pens, etc. and at a high price, but there is a severe shortage of essentials – food and clothing. I have bought myself a pipe! Everyone seems to speak English, even the hairdresser...

FAU, 205 Det. CA, Rear HQ 30 Corps, BLA [Natoye, Ardennes], 11 January 1945

We have now been split into five Sections as planned and I am at the address at the head of this letter, established with a 30 Corps Civil Affairs Detachment. Our team of eleven, actually ten, because Len Darling the Section Leader is still in hospital. The CA Det. has a Major in charge and three Captains – one British, one French-Canadian and a Dutch liaison officer who speaks several languages. Also a Dutch doctor and a British Red Cross doctor, two Dutch nurses, and six male and female Dutch civilians who act as interpreters and anything else that needs doing. They all eat with us in the officer's mess. There are numerous other ranks, all British Army who service the Detachment – drivers, cooks, etc. The Dutch civilians are all university students, so I don't suppose they will stay long, they had connections with the Dutch underground and it was thought their local knowledge would be useful. We have had some fascinating conversations with them as they all speak English and French, which is useful as we struggle with Walloon [sic] here. At first we were housed in a large monastery with reasonable sleeping accommodation. The officer's mess is where we all meet. The evening meal is a proper affair and we have to clean ourselves up beforehand, occasionally wine is served, and the conversation is friendly, even merry at times. Someone has obtained a liberated wireless, and the crusty old Major creases up laughing at 'Itma' *['It's That Man Again', a popular wartime radio programme]*, he seems to like us to listen with him. We also get daily papers, but they tend to be days late...

Since then we have moved forward again to another monastery, more primitive and still with a few monks living in it. It had been occupied by German troops who left a bit of a mess behind, and a richly decorated chapel which had been partly damaged by fire. We sleep in cells provided for the monks which are freezing, there is no heating in the whole building and we have to break the ice to shave in the mornings... Food is alright, now that the side roads have been cleared of snow and supplies allowed through. We are surrounded by snow covered, wooded hills, and to get around we have had to fit chains to the wheels of the vehicles, not so easy to fix or drive.

The British Army has advanced a little here and as a result we have had a number of refugee families coming in from the liberated villages,

Meeting 5 FAU in the Ardennes, January 1945 (George Champion)

cold and miserable dragging a few belongings with them, so pathetic. I have been assigned to help the two doctors with medical inspections, we are looking mainly for scabies, impetigo, head lice and so on which are very common, but very fortunately no sign of typhus. The Red Cross doctor is a bit on the lazy side, I think, anyway he leaves a lot to me, which I don't mind as I can do with the experience. He is rather fond of the whisky too! The Dutch doctor is young and very nice. When Holland was first invaded he was studying at Utrecht University, but was able to carry on and qualify, and then worked in a hospital. He became involved with the underground movement, and with two of the nurses, who are with us now, they were asked to hide four RAF air crew who had been shot down. In an extraordinary story they managed to help them escape to England by a small boat. When the British Army arrived in Holland he and the nurses offered their services, but he is hoping to join the newly formed Dutch forces. I get on well with him and have had some interesting conversations, even about me being a conchie. He said he belonged to a protestant church who also didn't believe in fighting, but I found this difficult to follow, although I gather he didn't get involved in sabotage but only on the medical side... Both our ambulances have just gone out on a call as we have been told there are some injured or ill civilians in a nearby village... One of the monks has asked the Red Cross doctor to have a look at his nose, as he thinks he has a boil or polyps, which will need to be lanced and has asked me to help him...

FAU, 205 Det. CA, Rear HQ 30 Corps [Château Rambeau, Ardennes], 22 Jan. 1945

Since I last wrote we have left the monastery and moved a little way back to a beautiful but quite modern chateau. What a change, marble floors, pillars, large high rooms, glass doors, you can well imagine. We understand it originally belonged to a very rich man who made his money in sugar. There is hot water with the expectation of baths in the near future. It was used by some high ranking German Army staff officers, but has been empty since they left. One of the caretakers, who lives nearby, told us that they took with them some of the large paintings, but there are still others on the walls.

We haven't set up the 'chain' as no refugees have come in since we arrived so we are enjoying a bit of a rest. I don't think I have ever described the 'chain' as we call the set up in which we work. In the building we find, to receive the refugees we usually try to have three medical inspection rooms, according to how many doctors are on duty, the FAU give general assistance, or take their place if they are not available. The

Studio portrait of Clifford, taken in Brussels

Sledging at Château Rambeau (George Champion)

refugee families are first registered by the Dutch nurses, then disinfested with DDT powder *[a white chlorinated hydrocarbon used as an insecticide]* before entering the MI rooms, and the nurses write down the doctor's findings. I help wherever needed and am also a reserve driver.

When the Section has to move we all help with the loading of the trucks with stores and equipment, it's hard work and takes time as we have over 14,000 lbs stores alone. We really need more transport and have asked for it. The 30cwt trucks are not big enough and we don't like putting too much in the ambulances in case they are needed... Some of us went tobogganing yesterday, which ended in a snow fight... Later we went wood collecting, and had a super log fire in the large open fireplace in the main room in the evening...

FAU. 205 Det. CA, Rear HQ 30 Corps [Château Rambeau, Ardennes], 1 Feb. 1945

We are still at the Chateau, but with very little to do, so we have put ourselves and the ambulances at the disposal of a local civilian hospital. It is much milder now and a big thaw is under way. While the snow and ice were bad enough the slush and mud aren't much better. We have all had the opportunity of a day off in Brussels, and on another occasion a party of us went to a nearby town to see an ENSA play – Cedric Hardwicke in 'Yellow Sands'. On the way back I called in to see Reg at 12 FSU, who are stationed quite near us, he goes on home leave next week. He had thought of asking for a transfer to our lot but has now decided against it. He is a relative new boy in the set up, most of the others are old campaigners who had served with Hadfield-Spears *[mobile hospital]* in Syria, the Western Desert, Tunisia, Italy and Southern France, and I think he feels he doesn't quite fit in. They were rather sniffy about our 'officer' status which they felt is out of keeping with FAU principles. I certainly don't see it that way, the nature of our work, quite different to theirs, requires us to be able to communicate and negotiate with both military and civilian officials, sometimes high up... Len Darling, the Section Leader, is back with us, he had pernicious anaemia, but is now fully recovered. He seems a nice chap. Eric Westwood *[not in our Section]* who was in hospital with him and had nephritis is returning to England... We have had fragments of news

Map of the front at this time, from an unidentified newspaper. Clifford marked a cross for their position between the two large arrows on the left near Dinant.

from one or two of the other FAU Sections. George Vaughan, a member of Stanley Hancock's Section 8, fractured his skull in a road accident and has been sent home, while the CA Detachment to which Ken Ford's Section 7 is attached came under fire and the Major and a Captain were killed. None of the FAU were hurt, although one of their ambulances was set on fire. Later, Islwyn Lake, he was in the 18th Training Camp with me, was captured by the Germans while out in his ambulance with a Dutch helper, picking up a sick woman. *[He remained a prisoner of war until just before the end of hostilities, when he managed to escape]*. Our Dutch doctor has now left us to take up a commission with Royal Dutch Army Medical Service. He would have preferred to have stayed with us but was put under some pressure, I gather. Before he left he gave me his address in Holland, just in case I was ever near there...

FAU, 205 Det. CA, Rear HQ 30 Corps, BLA [Château Rambeau, Ardennes], 6 Feb. 1945

We are still here but not for very much longer. The whole Detachment has been changed, which could herald a change to our activities. All our Dutch personnel have left and been replaced by a small group of RAMC men, it is rumoured that we cannot take Dutch civilians into Germany, so maybe that's where we are heading? ...there is great activity everywhere, which suggests we may be on the move soon... It's much milder and all the snow and ice have gone, but still much mud...

FAU, 205 Det. CA, Rear HQ 30 Corps, BLA [Wanroij, Holland], 11 February 1945

Since I last wrote we have had a long move northwards, and are in old army camp surrounded by barbed wire, not a very suitable place for refugees, as they could feel caged in, but it is obviously very temporary. Clearly there is a major offensive under way and the noise from the artillery is hardly conducive to sleep. We are trying to keep the road to the camp drained, but yesterday's work was completely undone by a column of tanks which churned it into a mud bath. It really isn't any fun when a three-ton lorry full of refugees gets stuck in it; one has to get them all off before we can try to free it. We really could do with more front-wheel drive trucks. Fortunately there aren't too many refugees, as most were evacuated from this area some weeks ago... We have been given to understand that we should prepare to go forward again at any time... You may like to know who my team mates are at present – Len Darling *[Section Leader]*, Dennis Wickham *[Deputy Section Leader]*, Harry Gaunt, Hugh Johns, David Curtis, George Champion, John Freshwater,

Gordon Taylor, Roger Stanger, Martin Southwood and myself, varying in age from 42 to 18, three are married and there is much family talk and swapping of snaps when the mail arrives. We do really get on very well together sharing the jobs and hardships... Sometimes I feel we are only nibbling at the problems, but then we are an emergency set up; it will be for others who follow to tackle the long term needs. When we get into Germany it may be different, the Army Civilian Affairs will become Military Government and as an all male organisation, at the moment, the FAU teams will be the only voluntary body allowed in while the fighting is going on. In any case the other bodies are more concerned with displaced persons and are bit reluctant to involve themselves with the German population at the moment... Although it was drizzling one or two of us went for a stroll in some woods near here, but what with blighted trees, destroyed sheds, discarded weapons, and occasional groups of wooden crosses, it was all rather depressing, and we had to be very watchful of landmines, although marked off with white tapes, no clearing is being done yet... I'll have to close now as the electric light goes off at ten.

FAU, 205 Mil. Gov., Rear HQ 30 Corps, BLA [Bedburg, Germany], 19 Feb. 1945

A very brief note just to let you know all is well. We have never been so busy with a really massive job on hand. We moved up from our last place through so much destruction and where we are now we are surrounded by hundreds of homeless, both displaced persons and German refugees. There are few usable buildings, no electricity and no uncontaminated water. There are going to be many hard days ahead, but I'll write when I can... I had a letter from Freda dated 9th Feb, but I had forgotten it was my birthday till I got it.

FAU, 205 Mil. Gov., Rear HQ 30 Corps, BLA [Bedburg, Germany], 25 Feb. 1945

The last few days have been hectic and not very pleasant. I did think twice about telling you, but as the dangerous bit seems to be mostly over, there is nothing to worry about. We travelled here through a very blighted forest [Reichswald, part of the Siegfried Line]. The roads were full of shell craters although some had been filled in with felled fir trees so vehicles could get across, and there was still some firing on all sides. The fighting was very recent as we saw destroyed tanks, some still burning, and in one instance a dead soldier half hanging out.

We arrived in this place, hardly a town more a settlement, a few hours after its capture, infantry were still 'mopping up'. It is very heavily damaged, I imagine there must have been some house to house fighting, and a haze of dust and a smell of cordite hanging in the air. We managed to find a not too damaged house, they were all unoccupied, and spent a very disturbed night 300 yards from the German positions. It was unnerving to see the streams of red hot tracer almost floating through the night and the constant loud crack of mortars firing and, occasionally, the rattling noise of Bren Gun carriers moving forward with the infantry. As soon as it was light we tried to assess the situation with the heavier artillery firing over our heads into the German positions. In the cellars of the mostly damaged houses and blocks of flats were hundreds of refugees, one or two with untreated wounds, many of whom had been there for four days, with only the food they had brought with them. Dead German and Canadian soldiers were still being buried. The plight of the refugees was terrible; we even helped a mother who was still looking for her children. It all seemed very daunting, how could we possibly cope? At least they could now come out into the fresh air, but with no electricity, water or food. The Detachment officers estimated there were about 6,000 people to cater for. But within 24 hours some water had been turned on, electricity from generators for part of the time, and food supplies coming in. Then just to make it worse the Luftwaffe paid us a visit, and the newspapers said the Luftwaffe was finished! David, Roger and myself were taking a look at a damaged building to see if it could be used as a temporary hospital when a plane dropped a bomb which fell, very fortunately, just outside the building. What was left of the windows came in and a bit more of the damaged roof was dislodged. We were knocked to the ground by the blast, but otherwise uninjured, although David had a slight cut on his nose, probably from a piece of flying glass.

This whole place, it had been a lunatic asylum for a 1,000 patients and there are still a large number here, has caught the imagination of the war correspondents, who are everywhere, including 'old Buckley' *[Christopher Buckley had been a history teacher at St Christopher School; he was later killed by a land mine during the Korean War]*, but he seemed a bit distracted and seemed unable to place me, his report appeared in the *Daily Telegraph* for 22nd February. We also had visits from a BBC wireless recording van and Gaumont British News, some of our chaps appeared in their shots. Watch out when you next see the news at the cinema... We are still being fed adequately, which is a bit embarrassing when we know how little the refugees are getting, although when fresh supplies don't come we have to make do with dry 'compo' rations...

I had a letter from Uncle Harry in which he said he had sent me

200 fags, wasn't that nice of him? I know I am smoking a bit too much, but we all do, even those who said they were strict non-smokers, maybe it's to do with the uncertain situation, anyway I expect we will revert to normality later...

FAU, 205 Mil. Gov., 30 Corps Rear HQ, BLA [Bedburg, Germany], 28 February 1945

I have found time to write a short note. Many thanks for your letter, Mummy, with the tobacco. I loved reading about the pond and the birds in the garden. It took twelve days before the birds came back here and started singing, and even those trees with branches blasted off, have a few little buds showing, it's wonderful. We are still very busy, but it is not so hectic, partly maybe because we are more organised! Refugees and displaced persons are coming in all the time as more areas are liberated, mostly having been directed to us by the Army. So many of the families seem to be incomplete. We have been told that Richard Wainwright's Section 5 is to take over from us and that we are to move forward to catch up with the forward units in the Army.

> Bedburg went on to become the largest temporary DP camp in Germany with over 20,000 people.

FAU, 205 Mil. Gov., Rear HQ 30 Corps, BLA [Kochinoff, near Goch, Germany], 5 March 1945

Many thanks for the letters, it was nice to have your news. Interested to hear about the 'Save the Woods' campaign, and that Edward Barnard & Sons are doing well. Sheila [Wilton, girlfriend from schooldays] wrote to say she was at the English Goethe Society and thought Dorothy Sayers spoke very well. She thought she saw you, Daddy, but wasn't too sure, I've told her to talk to you on the next occasion. Have a nice break at Jordans at Easter. Well, as you will see from the address we have moved forward again. When we arrived at the field allocated to us by the Army we were told the German positions were in some trees only about a field away, so we were told to dig well in! But nothing happened and they pulled out during the night. For the first time we had to dig a hole in the ground and put a tent over the top in case it rained, quite snug actually. Coping with refugees who are all under canvas is another whole ball game, and the fields are a quagmire. Fortunately, the Detachment army personnel help put up the many tents that were needed. We saw some planes diving to attack some positions less than a mile away two days ago. We are mostly having to deal with displaced persons now, largely those who

Kochinoff camp (George Champion)

were forced to work in Germany and now want to get home. However there are some Russians who don't want to go back, and also many Poles who would rather remain in Germany. That is going to be a problem for the future. I have noticed one unusual thing, the Ukrainians get very uptight if you call them Russian and are very nationalistic...

FAU, 205 Mil. Gov., Rear HQ 30 Corps, BLA [Kochinoff, south of Goch], 17 March 1945

Sorry, I haven't written for some time, but I have had several other letters to do, including Uncle Harry and Auntie Hilda, who both sent me 200 fags. Many thanks for the Nivea cream, shaving soap and tobacco, but my pipe has broken and I can't smoke till I get another... As fast as we get the DPs away more come in – mainly Russians and Poles, but also Dutch, French and Latvians, Lithuanians, Yugoslavs, Italians, Czechs, one Greek and one who insisted on being registered as an American/ Pole. Despite all their difficulties the Russians seem a gay lot, an endless source of amusement, singing and dancing into the small hours, and lighting small fires, which are not allowed because of the danger of setting fire to the tents. We have had to ask the help of some British soldiers to make them put them out. Problems, but nothing to compare with the place we have just left, where we understand numbers have now reached over 20,000, and as the farms are mostly deserted the cattle still left alive have been rounded up and corralled in fields near the camp, so they can be milked and looked after! Things are much quieter,

very occasional shelling but a long way away and a few planes screech-
ing across the sky often very low so as to be able to see their markings of
both sides… I have had a bit of a cold, but it's cleared up now, being in
the outdoors is probably a good thing… Thank you for your letter Freda,
and very best wishes for your wedding anniversary – can hardly believe
you have been married for a year…

FAU, 205 Mil. Gov., Rear HQ 30 Corps, BLA [Kochinoff, south of Goch], 26 March 1945

I've just come back from a 48 hour leave *[in Brussels]*. The weather was
really warm and most people were in summery clothes. I went with Gordon and we tried the opera but were not impressed, it was *Boris Godunov*,
also the cinema, had ice creams and coffees in street cafes, all so civilised,
it was so surprising to see how quickly things are getting back to normal.
We stayed in an officer's club, previously a hotel, and had hot baths, slept
in beds with clean sheets, and put our shoes outside the door at night to
be cleaned! It was so strange to be rubbing shoulders with colonels and
majors, sipping iced beer in a palm tree lounge while an orchestra played

*Hundreds of thousands of these leaflets with various calendar girls were
dropped by the Luftwaffe over the British and American lines in March 1945
following the collapse of the German Army's last advance in the Ardennes
just before Christmas.*

dance music. On the Sunday morning we walked in the Royal Park, with wonderful sunshine, and watched the squirrels and small boys sailing their boats in the large lake. It was all so peaceful and the war seemed hundreds of miles away. For a short time we watched a football match between England and Belgium, but had to leave half way through to fetch our bags and join our truck for the journey through the night back to our Section. While there I went bust and bought a nice briar pipe to replace my cracked one, it cost 200 francs. The Detachment personnel are in high spirits as the military news is good and things seem to really be going our way now...

The DPs are not in very good shape and we have found lice, so have set up a bath unit, quite a feat to get a water supply going, we called in an Army bath unit... Yes, we do see Gerald Gardiner *[overall leader of all the FAU teams in Germany]* from time to time, he makes regular visits to all the Sections, and Len Darling is back after his leave, he is a good leader with grasp of any situation. It must be hard for him with so many of us youngsters in his team...

After the war Len became a teacher and Gerald, a barrister by training, was appointed Lord Chancellor by Harold Wilson in 1964. During his time in office capital punishment was abolished, and laws regarding abortion and homosexuality were reformed. He appointed the first woman judge to the High Court and introduced a compulsory training programme for Justices of the Peace.

FAU, 205 Mil. Gov., Rear HQ 30 Corps, BLA [Groin, in the Rees Bridgehead over the Rhine, Germany], 2 April 1945

You will have to guess were we are now, but that shouldn't be difficult. It's been a lively time with some hairy driving involved *[particularly the narrow pontoon bridge over the Rhine; and see Introduction p.15 for shrapnel incident]*. We had to go into our holes for one night, but the front moved away very quickly. Again many DPs and German refugees with lice but no typhus thank goodness. But there is clearly a food shortage for the local populace... We had a fresh boiled egg for Easter as we found many hens running about loose on a vacant farm, so we helped ourselves...

FAU, 205 Mil. Gov., Rear HQ 30 Corps, BLA [Lingen, Germany] 11 April 1945

Things are moving very quickly now, with little resistance from the German Army. We have had to move three times to keep up. No sooner have

Football at Lingen (George Champion)

we got set up when we have to pack up again, we've done more of this than coping with DPs and refugees. Our first stop was at an agricultural research station owned by a branch of the Krupps family, then at a stud farm, but there were no horses, and now we are in a large ex-German Army barracks. Because we have moved so often we haven't had any post for some time... the weather has been super, really quite warm for the time of year... By the way the magazine *Illustrated* for 7 April carries an article and photos of where we were when we first entered Germany *[Bedburg]*. The Mil. Gov. Detachment referred to is ours, but the FAU are not named... We get few German refugees now, as the towns are little damaged and people are staying in their homes. Mixed in with the DPs we are getting quite a number of prisoners of war, so some Stalags must have been liberated, mostly French, Italian and Polish. The German population are not openly hostile, more sullen and uncommunicative, not very sure of what is going to happen – a few more friendly glances now and again...

FAU, 205 Mil. Gov., 30 Corps Rear HQ, BLA [Holzhausen, off the Harpstedt–Bassum Road, Germany], 19 April 1945

Another long hop since I last wrote, well east of the Rhine which we crossed four weeks ago now. We are administering another large tented camp for DPs, there is no longer a problem with German refugees... In answer to your question we get anyone we can to do our laundry for cigarettes or money, we supply the soap, any mending we do ourselves.

FAU, 205 Det. Mil. Gov., Rear HQ 30 Corps, BLA [Holzhausen, Germany], 26 April 1945

I was fascinated to read the accounts of the Rhine crossing and the subsequent battles in Germany from the papers you sent, most interesting to get an overall perspective of something we have been living through. The article 'Desert Germany' in the *New Statesman* seems to reciprocate what I have seen and feel. I shared it with others here and we feel the immediate outlook for Germany is not promising. In several areas we are finding ourselves at odds with the Allied Authorities policy. They require that all DPs must be fed from German food stocks, one can see the reasoning – Germans brought them here, so Germans can feed them – but the stocks in some areas are already non-existent, and the policy simply can not be sustained. They seem to turn a blind eye to all the looting by soldiers and ex-slave workers and raping. Many Germans don't seem to be aware of what was done during their occupation of Russia, Poland and so on, and can't see why they should be so hated and think they are the only ones to be treated badly. There is going to be a great need for a carefully worded education programme, but we don't see anything like this getting underway for a long time. Some of the DPs can't understand why we won't go out with them on looting or beating up parties. We do our best to explain our position, but our hands are tied as we have no means or authority to prevent them from leaving the camp. But we have to stay and just compromise and hope we can play some more enlightened part later. We had to arrange for milk supplies for the DPs from a local farm, as we approached the farmhouse we saw the locked and barred doors and shuttered windows, and when the door was finally opened their grim frightened faces. But we tried to arrange what we had to in as a

2 FAU at crossroads, Harpstedt, the sign clearly showing 27 Km to Bremen which was still in German hands. The soldier on a bicycle had come to warn us not to turn left as the road ran straight in to the German positions. Left to right: Arthur Jewson, Hugh Johnes, Dennis Wickham. (George Champion)

Overnight stay at Holzhausen (George Champion)

friendly a way as possible, explaining they would be recompensed from the local German authorities, and point out that feeding the DPs in camp meant fewer would wish to go out and loot. We promised that the milk would always be fetched by us and left with smiles on their faces. As so often before the fact that they can see we don't carry guns seems to help.

You ask if our work will end with the cessation of hostilities, no I think it will be just a beginning of another phase. Many of the western DPs will soon return home, but there will have to be camps or whatever for those eastern DPs who don't want to go home, and then what can we do to help the Germans rehabilitate themselves and embrace a more democratic society. Some of the Mil. Gov. Officers are surprisingly enlightened and I am sure we can work with them.

We have been receiving reports of the uncovering of a concentration camp by the British Army with terrible conditions – many dead and dying and typhus widespread, we expect to hear more... Yes, we have had news of Islwyn Lake. He was in a camp when the Germans started to take the prisoners to Denmark, but he asked to stay so that he and a Dutch doctor could care for those too ill to travel. As British troops approached he managed to get away in a car and reported back at his Section one morning for work! They sent him back to England.

4. Sandbostel
Concentration Camp

May 1945

The next two letters were the only ones I wrote from Sandbostel concentration camp. The main reason for not writing more often was due, I guess, because we were occupied from morning to night, only taking time to sleep when we could, but partly, perhaps, because I found it difficult to find what to say that would not have added to my parents' anguish with more unpleasant details. The letters, of course, only give my immediate reactions to what I was experiencing, and it was not until I started researching, many years later, for my book *Two Weeks in May 1945* that I discovered many more of the facts of what had happened. I spent considerable time in the Public Records Office at Kew, the Imperial War Museum library and elsewhere, perusing diaries, letters, army records and reports, and books, sometimes finding I had to try and reconcile conflicting information. My research also corrected some of the conjectures in my letters.

As the episode is central to my experiences in these letters and probably the one of most interest to readers, I thought it would be appropriate to include some background here in a précis of the information given in that book. For further observations, see the revised version of *Sandbostel Revisited* on pages 171–191.

Sandbostel Camp was situated on a stretch of bare and bleak heath land about eight miles south of Bremervörde, with a small road running past the entrance. It comprised many large and smaller barrack-like wooden buildings, surrounded by tall barbed wire fences with watch towers. There were three sections. The first and second accommodated some fifteen thousand prisoners of war. The first was mostly for French, British and Canadian soldiers, where the conditions were very basic, but they had, as far as we could discover, been treated within the terms of the International Red Cross Convention, although some in the Camp hospital were in a poor condition and should have had better medical attention. Those in the second section, mainly Russian soldiers, who without the protection of the Convention had fared much worse, being fed far less food than the Westerners. But even here the conditions could not compare in any way with the appalling situation that was found in the third section – a concentration camp for some eight thousand 'political' prisoners of many nationalities.

The British Army had known for some time that there was a prisoner of war camp at Sandbostel – Stalag XB – but were not aware of the separate compound with political prisoners whose plight was desperate. The inmates had arrived only four weeks before, from Neuengamme, a long established concentration camp near Hamburg. They were transported in cattle trucks for eight days without food or water, and although the train was constantly stopping no one was allowed to disembark, nor dispose of those who had died, and the conditions became horrific. Finally they had to march two kilometres, to be dumped in part of the Stalag, despite the protests of the German Camp Commandant. The SS guards allowed nobody, not even the German Camp doctor, to enter this separate compound. The distressing news of their predicament was brought by two PoWs, an Englishman and a Frenchman, who managed to escape and make their way to the British lines. Despite being heavily engaged with the retreating German forces, the decision was made to divert troops and liberate the camp at once, which involved a dangerous assault over the river Oste incurring casualties, but the Camp was overrun on the evening of 29 April. As the British Army approached most of the SS and German Army guards withdrew, and those who remained handed their weapons and the responsibility over to the French Commandant in charge of the PoWs, but there was little that could be done until the British troops arrived.

On the morning of 30 April Captain Robert Barer, an RAMC doctor, became the first officer of the liberating forces to enter the Camp. After making contact with the cheering PoWs and reassuring them that help was on its way, he went through the whole compound occupied by the political prisoners. Later in graphic detail he described in a Report* how he passed a forbidding notice over the entrance *Danger Typhus – Keep Out* and 'entered hut after hut, through dark passages, over floorboards rotted through and slimy with filth, stumbling over bodies, mostly dead'. During the night the Royal Engineers completed building a bridge over the river, and in the morning Captain Barer was able to arrange for an

---

*Captain Robert Barer, MC RAMC, 'Report on Sandbostel Concentration Camp, 1945' in *One Young Man and Total War – from Normandy to Concentration Camp: A Doctor's Letters Home* (Durham: Pentland Press, 1998), pp. 276–285.

RAMC Field Ambulance Unit and Field Hygiene Section to be brought up to start the rescue operation.

An overwhelming task confronted these small contingents. The official Army medical history* recorded

> ...in the compound occupied by the political prisoners the conditions were utterly horrifying. In hutted accommodation, adequate maybe for about 2,000, were between 7,000 and 8,000 emaciated males of fifteen years and upwards. The great majority of them were in a deplorable state of malnutrition. Starved and gravely ill men in filthy rags lay huddled on the bare floors. Everywhere the dead and dying sprawled amid slime of human excrement...

The Light Field Ambulance Unit, which was so crucial to the whole operation, had only 10 officers (one not a doctor) and 112 other ranks. They had the support of two German military doctors, six civilian German doctors, 66 German nurses and 185 civilian women. Many other German civilians were brought in from the surrounding towns and villages over the next few days, including a large group of high school girls, and on 6 May, the Light Field Ambulance Unit was reinforced by an RAMC Casualty Clearing Station. A 'human laundry', modelled on the one used at Belsen concentration camp, which had been uncovered a few days before, was set up with twenty tables. Inmates were brought in at the dirty end, clothing such as it was removed and burnt, and all hair-bearing areas shaved. Then they were taken to another table for complete washing with soap and water, dried and dusted with DDT, wrapped in a clean blanket, placed on a stretcher and carried to an improvised 'hospital' – a group of wooden buildings in rather better condition, that had been cleaned for the purpose. From 1 to 6 May some 300 patients were transferred each day; this was later raised to 400.

Around 100 inmates continued to die every day, but by 9 May this had been reduced to about twenty. Some 400 impressed German civilians were kept busy removing the dead bodies from the huts and burying them in large pits without ceremony as there was no means of knowing who they were or where they came from. With the end of hostilities on 8 May it was possible to move 86 British General Hospital to Rotenburg, about 20 miles from Sandbostel, and from 11 May they were able to take patients from the improvised Camp hospital. Now, however, inmates who had been walking about a few days earlier started going down

*The Medical History of the Second World War: The Army Medical Services (Campaigns); vol.iv North-West Europe, edited by F.A.E. Crew (London: HMSO, 1962).

with typhus, so every bed possible was needed, and tents erected in the spaces between the huts were soon filled. Slowly, however, all the huts were cleared and the patients transferred to the 'hospitals'. Convalescent camps were set up in Seedorf and Farge, first for walking patients and then for those who could be released from hospitalisation, but the last patients did not leave the Camp until 6 June.

When the Army were first made aware of the Camp at Sandbostel, an order was sent to 205 Det. Mil. Gov. to make for the Camp at all haste. Following a request the FAU team, who were working with the Det., readily agreed to accompany them. Stores and equipment were hurriedly packed up and arrangements made for the DP camp which we had been running to be taken over by another team. After a hazardous and tiring drive through part of the night and most of the next day, over bomb-cratered roads and long waits to cross temporary river bridges, and avoiding areas still occupied by German forces, the convoy finally arrived at Sandbostel on the evening of 1 May, the day after the Camp had first been entered. The Army made 205 Det. Mil. Gov. responsible for obtaining as much food stuffs as possible from local sources, and to procure all the stores, equipment and clothing as it was requested, a vast undertaking. Some members of the FAU team helped with this work, some supervised groups of women in the 'human laundry', while others organised the feeding arrangements in the large kitchen. Carefully worked-out diet scales provided by the RAMC doctors were used. Six days later we were relieved from running the kitchen when personnel from the Casualty Clearing Station arrived on 6 May. The FAU team left the Camp on 16 May to run the convalescent camp we had established at Farge, which was now full.

FAU, 205 Det. Mil. Gov., Rear HQ 30 Corps, BLA [Sandbostel Concentration Camp, south of Bremevörde], 3 May 1945

The last few days have been distressing and very unpleasant, and we are still trying to come to terms with what we have experienced. Shortly after I wrote my last letter at the DP camp we received a very urgent movement order and had to hurriedly pack up and move out the same afternoon. We had a fair way to go and due to the damaged state of the roads and the difficulty of trying to find our way in the dark without headlights, travel was rather slow, and we ended up having to spend the night on the Bremen–Hamburg autobahn *[we had to be careful not to go too far along the road as Hamburg and the area around was still in German hands]* trying to get some sleep in the cabs or backs of our vehicles, eerily there was not sight nor sound of any other traffic. We arrived at our rendezvous, an advanced post, the following morning to be told our job was to help 'clear up' a joint PoW and concentration camp, which was still in the process of being freed of the German troops surrounding it. Following an earlier escape of two PoWs something was known of the prevailing conditions and that typhus was widespread. We understood that a truce had been arranged with the camp guards and the British units were now able to move in. *[This was not entirely accurate and I never did discover the truth of the arrangement that was made, but more about this is to be found in* Two Weeks in May 1945.*]* We found there were two distinct camps, one for PoWs and one for 'political' prisoners. There are some 14,000 PoWs, including some 350 British and Canadian soldiers, and 7,500 in the concentration camp. The conditions in the PoW section were very basic but they had been fed, although the Russian soldiers in a separate section had been treated worse than the others. Was this because the USSR had not signed the Geneva Convention, I wonder? In no way, however, did this compare with the conditions in the concentration camp which were beyond belief. Very many unburied dead lying all over the place and living dead crawling through the muck, mostly brought about through starvation and illness – typhoid, typhus and TB. There had been no food whatsoever for the last 8 or 9 days, and it was estimated that 150 inmates were dying every day. *[Other accounts give different figures.]* A fearful stench, impossible to describe, drifted everwhere, and there was no sanitation whatsoever.

There was much to be done but difficult to know where to start. An RAMC Field Ambulance unit had been brought in, to direct operations, and as many local German doctors and nurses as could be found were rounded up. Every day several hundred civilians from surrounding towns and villages were transported in, to stretcher bear the weak but still living, to carry the dead bodies and throw them in to the large pits that had been dug, and to start cleaning the place up. Each living inmate is fed a sort of soup until they are considered strong enough to be passed through the 'human laundry'. Clothes are removed and burnt, then they are washed and powdered with DDT, head shaved, wrapped in a blanket, and put in a bunk bed in one of the barrack buildings which have been cleaned, or tents which had hurriedly been erected. Where they are then fed on a specially worked out diet and vitamin tablets. We are able to say that the death rate is now down to some 10 or 15 a day, and the whole contaminated area was finally cleared this morning. We are told that the dirty huts will be burnt down. Our job has been mainly the feeding of those political prisoners who can still walk in what has been termed Camp 2 – huts that had not before been used for prisoners, but had been quarters for the guards, or used as offices, stores, etc.

All the food has to be found and brought in. A kitchen has been cleaned and partly re-equipped with large cauldrons to make soup. Martin Southwood has been put in charge with the help of teams of German women. British soldiers are on guard, as at one time, when food was first brought in, it looked as though the walking prisoners would storm it, and also for the protection of the German women.

The PoW camp is Stalag XB. On the first day we found time to talk to one or two of the British soldiers, but they are all gone now. They had dozens of questions and couldn't wait to get home, some had been prisoners for several years, others only for a matter of weeks...

Gerald Gardiner paid us a visit and brought some news and a special letter from Tegla Davies at FAU HQ in London, which is being sent to all FAU teams everywhere. I thought you might like to know what he had to say so I have written it out here –

> The war in Europe may soon be over. An armistice will be the occasion not only for services of thanksgiving – and the pacifist will have as much cause for thanksgiving as anyone – but for victory celebrations and revelry on a grand scale. Such victory celebrations will take place publicly; they will also be held privately, probably in every hospital or other centre in which the Unit works. It will be easy to be carried along by mass enthusiasm. On behalf of the Executive and Advisory Committee, I need to do no more than ask members to show discretion and not, at the last stage of the war, to give an impression of invalidating the stand which they have made since it began. I am not asking that Sections should not celebrate the end of five years of war, many will wish to do so; let it be in the right way and for the right reasons. That is different from celebrating victory. Nor should we be lacking in understanding and give offence to those who, having for so long pursued the war with sincerity and devotion will find emotions unleashed which we cannot share. We cannot share in celebrations of military victory. Let our prevailing mood be one of thanksgiving that the war is over and dedication to the cause of peace. And let our conduct fit our mood.

FAU, 205 Det. Mil. Gov., Rear HQ 30 Corps, BLA [Sandbostel Concentration Camp], 10 May 1945

...I enclose a cutting from the Daily Telegraph so you will know exactly where I am...

It is now five days since the 'cease fire' was declared on the 21st Army Group front, so life is strangely peaceful... only just before German artillery had still been shelling occasionally and the bridge behind the camp was hit, which was our only line of communication out of the camp as the German positions were less than 2 miles in front of us... There has been surprisingly little celebration among the British troops round here, although some Scottish soldiers in the front line have been shooting Very lights in the air… according to the wireless there seems to be far more jollity in England. The one topic of conversation among the Det. soldiers is when can we get home? There are many rumours in the air about the future of the FAU, but it is all largely speculation, however, it is still a bit early as there is clearly still much to be done here, and, of course, in the longer term, also among the German population themselves.

A store of around 3,500 Red Cross parcels, which had been intended for distribution to British POWs, has been uncovered. These were meant for individual use – small packets and little tins, and chocolate bars, so every parcel has to be opened and unpacked and all the little lots sorted into like groups so they can be taken to the kitchen to make meals for prisoners. The cigs. are being kept back for later use… All that the ill prisoners were wearing had to be burnt, so vast amounts of replacement clothing had to be brought in from local towns, greatly helped by the discovery of a barge on the river filled with uniforms. If it wasn't for the tragedy of it one would have to smile at the comic figures some of them make in their ill-fitting uniforms, but at least they are clean and warm… The PoW camp is now almost empty, with only Polish and Yugoslav soldiers left behind, as they don't wish to go home… Interested to read about the plans for WGC *[Welwyn Garden City]* after the war… and I have heard that the petrol ration has now been restored, that was quick. I suppose a car will be out of my reach for some time when I finally get home!

FAU, 205 Det. Mil. Gov., Rear HQ 30 Corps, BLA [Farge, Weser estuary, Germany], 16 May 1945

…I was interested to hear of all the goings on at home on VE Day…and particularly to have Daddy's impressions of unreality on the end of the war in Europe, I think I felt similarly at first. I had been hopeful of something good coming out of the San Francisco Conference *[an international conference held April–June 1945: the representatives of 47 nations met to draw up the charter of the United Nations]* despite the obvious difficulties of the Polish question, but I think I will now have to share your more pessimistic views. Obviously, a spontaneous arrangement arising from the people of various nations would be far and away the best, but there are no signs of that happening, and the 'Big Five', who have the actual power to make change, will dominate… The DPs with whom I have been able to talk just a little, mainly in broken German or English, don't seem to have any idea of the immensity of the post-war problems, only wanting a very hard peace for Germany, but then they are ones that have suffered… At the moment our team is split in two, four of our team and some Det. personnel have moved to Farge, on the Weser estuary, near Bremen. In an old barrack hospital, part of an old Kriegsmarine Lager *[Navy Camp]*, we have set up a sort of convalescent home for some of the fitter ex-inmates from Sandbostel. The hospital was well staffed and fully equipped with beds, etc., with only some 100 patients, so we have moved 600 ex-Sandbostel into a going concern and the kitchen is already turning out food for them. We have made ourselves comfortable in a spare part of the staff quarters with beds and hot water!

...Adjoining the hospital was another terrible place, a sort of underground factory, with the remains of Nazi SS goings on and signs of their very rapid departure, there was some damage and it would appear they had to try to burn a part of the place before they left. From what we have learned the 'slave' labourers worked and lived underground, almost like pit ponies. An underground waterway connects with a 'U' boat pen in the estuary, maybe the 'factory' was also a maintenance depot for submarines. The structures are very solid and bomb proof... It is such a strange feeling to see German soldiers and sailors in smart uniforms walking about in Bremen who will insist on saluting us. I suppose they are waiting to be demobilised. German police are now directing the traffic, including British Army vehicles, through the streets, practical really, but it does feel odd... The weather is really hot at the moment and we would love to swim in the estuary, but have been advised not to, for a number of reasons... Army regulations now allow battle-dress tops to be left off, and for officers to wear shirts and ties provided that braces don't show and clean webbing belts to be worn. We will follow suit in our own way! ... Some welcome news, 30 Corps HQ have recognised 205 Det.'s hard work at Sandbostel and is allowing us a 5 day rest in a suitable place to start at the end of the present job.

FAU, 205 Det. Mil. Gov., Rear HQ 30 Corps, BLA [Farge], 21 May 1945

Many thanks for your letters and the packet of papers. The liberal minded article on the 'horror' camps and the plan for Europe in *Picture Post,* were particularly interesting, also the letters in response in the following issue show some people are thinking internationally. I find the Citizen's Diary in the *Welwyn Times* very amusing, the fellow is a bit of a wit... We are still occupied with the convalescent hospital for ex-inmates of Sandbostel at Farge, which incidentally is on the east bank of the Weser, north of Bremen. As the place was almost running itself, with little for us to do, it was decided that half the team should take the opportunity of the five day rest which had been allocated to us. I was in the first party and we drove to Cuxhaven, a seaside resort on the North Sea. It was in the area that surrendered so did not experience the fighting and is virtually undamaged. We were billeted in a house where a woman who was living alone was prepared to cook the rations we had brought with us. We made the most of the time we had, swimming in the sea and sunning ourselves on the beach. *[Little did I know then how well I was going to get to know the place in happier times.]* One day we went to the river Oste, above Neuhaus, and took out boats to sail or row. The Major took Len off to shoot wild fowl. We all got rather sunburnt from the salt air as we were rowing with only our soccer pants on! Cuxhaven is still full of German soldiers and sailors striding about, the officers still seem to have saloon cars. What a difference to the British Tommy, who we saw sitting on the sea wall watching the waves in his shirt sleeves and smoking his pipe, oblivious to all around him... We returned today to learn that the Bremen area is to be taken over as an enclave for the American Army. So we will have to move again.

For further information and reflections on Sandbostel, see pp.171–91.

5. Hesslingen to Otterndorf

May to August 1945

FAU, 205 Det. Mil. Gov., Rear HQ 30 Corps, BLA
[Hesslingen, Germany], 28 May 1945

The American Army took over the Bremen area, as we had expected, and we had little to do except service our vehicles for four days. We then moved a long way south to Hesslingen, about 15 miles north-east of Braunschweig, into an area controlled by the US 9th Army, but we understand the British Army will be taking over soon. The area has quite a history. Once only heathland, it was turned into a Nazi KDF Stadt (Kraft durch Freude = Strength through Joy) to service the Volkswagen factory – the manufacturers of the People's Car. It was supposed to be a model town with modern flats for the workers with all social amenities, but to me it seems very unfinished with very drab block buildings. There is supposed to be around 20,000 German inhabitants now. When war production started many foreign workers were forcibly drafted in and housed in rather less comfortable conditions. Consequently the place has now become a vast DP camp. In one barrack camp there are hundreds of ex-Italian PoWs waiting for repatriation. Overall there are some 24,000 DPs, but as soon as some are moved out others are brought in. All the Westerners are being quickly sent home, but the Poles and Russians are static. It is strange that up to now the Soviet Government has showed little interest in all their Russian nationals in Germany, but this is probably only temporary. The Poles are adamant that they won't return to their homeland until the Russian Army, at present in occupation, leave. So that's going to be a problem, and makes a mockery of the statement by a 30 Corps Colonel that all DP repatriation would be over by March 1946… Apart from those DPs already in the Hesslingen transit camp, there are believed to be several thousands more in the surrounding countryside, all are due to be brought in to be registered and examined before being allowed to go home. How long is that going to take us?…

We have learnt a little more about our own future. Under British Army demobilisation plans, conchies will be released only after their equivalent Army group has been completed. Groups up to number 23 should have gone by December. My equivalent Army age group is 56 which at the present rate could be another two years to come up! Plans for home leave are bit more definite. This will start in July with married men first, I reckon I could be eligible late in August. You mention that you had read that General Horrocks *[Commander of 30 Corps]* is arranging for his men to have leave in Denmark. I haven't heard of this. I did meet him once he seemed a very unassuming man, when he visits his units he does it alone without the usual retinue. When he came to visit Sandbostel he asked especially to see Len Darling, shook hands with him and asked him to convey his thanks to us all... Interested to learn that Tegla Davies spoke at Yearly Meeting, I would like to have heard him... Rather surprised that Friends Relief Service teams were delayed coming out here because they could not agree to abide by the non-fraternisation rule. I have to say it is a policy which while made much of publicly is only patchily practised on the ground. You only have to walk around after dark to see groups of soldiers chatting quite freely to German girls with no apparent hindrance from the Military Police. We have long had Mil. Gov.'s permission to carry German civilians in our vehicles officially on business, and obviously have to converse with many different local officials. It is not really a very practical policy and will, I think, have to be rescinded soon...

I had a letter from Gaydu the other day; he is now Second Lieutenant Gayward of the Yorkshire Hussars! *[Gaydu had a Jewish father and an Aryan mother and was considered of 'mixed race' by the Nazi authorities. He came to England just before the war started, aged 12, his mother somehow getting him on a list of children to flee Vienna, very surprisingly not by the Kindertransport, but by air. Gaydu was one of several refugee children taken in by Lyn Harris, the headmaster of St Christopher School, where I met and befriended him. His father died in an asylum following a breakdown, Gaydu never knew the circumstances but had reason to fear the worst. His mother survived and Gaydu met her again after an interval of seven years in 1947. He told his story in an article in the St Christopher Club Newsletter No.43, January 2009.]* Also heard from David Grensted *[one time head boy at St Christopher]*, he wanted to know all about Germany from the inside...

I have noticed a rather interesting development; quite a number of factories in the American sector are already being repaired and in some cases put back into production. For example, the Volkswagen factory, where we are now, which was liberated by the Americans, is already turning out 12 cars a day. Will this continue when it comes under British jurisdiction? There are few signs of similar activity in the British

Zone, although it has to be said that the damage in the Ruhr, which is the largest industrial area in the zone, is so comprehensive it will surely take much longer to rehabilitate, and we have had reports that in some cases workable machinery is being taken away to other countries. This is being done on an even larger scale in the Russian Zone. Is this official looting, or considered legitimate reparations? Some of our Section had occasion to meet with an UNRRA *[United Nations Relief and Rehabilitation Association]* team the other day, several of whom were Americans, whose main qualification seemed to be that they had experience of business. Could this have any bearing I wonder? There is another UNRRA team in the area that is here to look into problems of DPs, but they decline to have anything to do with the Russian DPs. I wonder what's behind that?

FAU, 205 Det. Mil. Gov., Rear HQ 30 Corps, BLA
[Hesslingen], 3 June 1945
The British Army has now taken over here and the Americans have left. Very hot with periodic thunderstorms – continental climate, I suppose. It is rumoured that all voluntary bodies in the Second Army area will in future have to work under the auspices of UNRRA, but at the moment we are simply carrying on as before. The older members of the team, who are fairly near demob anyway, would like to see a complete cessation of FAU

Tangermünde: the destroyed bridge can be seen on the left (Gordon Taylor)

work, rather than try to do it, probably in a different way, under UNRRA supervision. We shall have to see how things develop... A further 20 FAU members were sent out two weeks ago to act as medical orderlies in the concentration camps. But most of this kind of work is already over and in any case the RAMC had things well in hand, so it was decided that they should be dispersed among the FAU teams already here. Four have joined our team, which makes us 16, the largest we have ever been, but some of the older ones will be due for demob soon... Good news, home leave is to be 10 days every four months instead of six, we still get four 48 hours leave a year... I wonder if Freda *[my sister was a primary school teacher]* would like to see the enclosed children's' drawings, I found them in a bombed school. I reckon the children would have been around 7 to 8. As you will see the pictures are all of German planes shooting down British planes. Did the teacher encourage them to draw such pictures, I wonder?... I gather general election fever has started over there – I would like to see a Labour majority with Cripps as Prime Minister!

FAU, 205 Det. Mil. Gov., Rear HQ 30 Corps, BLA [Tangermünde, Germany], 9 June 1945

Well, we have moved as far east as we can get. Right to the Elbe, to Tangermünde, south-east of Stendal, from our billets we can see the river and on the far bank the troops of the Red Army! It has its place in recent

The temporary bridge; a tiny dot in the distance is the Red Army's star

history, as it was here that 70,000 German troops, fleeing from the Russian advance, left their burnt out military vehicles on the east bank, crossed over and surrendered to just *five* American soldiers, blowing the only surviving bridge behind them. In a way our job is going to be a bit historic too, for we are establishing a small transit camp for Russian DPs and ex-POWs where they can sleep for a night, before crossing the river on their long journey home. We will receive a few Westerners in return. As the railway bridge was completely destroyed a narrow pontoon bridge was constructed, which has been decorated with bunting and flags, and sentries placed at both ends. Half the bridge is painted red and the other half red, white and blue, with a barrier in the middle. It is forbidden for British or Russian soldiers to cross into each other's territory.

The town of Tangermünde must be one of the prettiest German towns I have seen so far. It stands at the confluence of the rivers Elbe and Tanger, and is a river port for small ships, barges, and so on, but not enough industrialisation to spoil its character. There are delightful cobbled streets leading down to the river bank and half timbered buildings with green bottled glass windows. The shops have beautiful wooden carved signs hanging over their doorways. At one time it was

Displaced Persons at Tangermünde (Gordon Taylor)

a walled city and several semi-ruined arches and small towers can still be seen.The only thing that's missing is the stork's nest on the roof of the Rathaus... In answer to your question, Daddy, I can't say I have heard any Plattdeutsch *[Low German]* spoken, not that I would recognise it if I did. My knowledge of German is so basic that I haven't noticed any difference in dialect since we left the Rhine, sorry. *[My father had a degree in German, and took as his thesis some aspects of the dialect of the Frisian Islands]*

FAU, 205 Det. Mil. Gov., Rear HQ 30 Corps, BLA [Tangermünde], 15 June 1945

Little news, still processing the Russians returning home, but far fewer numbers now. All a bit routine, but we are cheerful and well... I tried out a local hairdresser the other day, and in the course of conversation discovered he could speak Plattdeutsch, but he said it was hardly ever spoken in the area, as the influence of other dialects was stronger. A man was there who had come from Berlin, and said the bombing had been so terrible, that he had had to leave. I asked after the Olympic Stadium and Potsdam Palace which I saw in 1936. He said the first was bombed flat and the second gutted by fire, I hope he was only exaggerating... Gerald Gardiner paid us a visit. He had just returned from a Mediterranean conference of FAU leaders in Rome. News on home leave is that it will start in July. Six of our number are now due but only one can go at a time, so we drew a ballot for a rota, I came third. As we get 10 days each, and bearing the travelling time, I reckon my turn could be in August...

FAU, 205 Det. Mil. Gov., Rear HQ 30 Corps, BLA [Tangermünde], 24 June 1945

It has been rumoured that the British, American and French Armies are being allowed zones in Berlin with communication corridors through Russian occupied territory. In compensation the Russians will move the boundary of their zone of occupation further west, which means they will soon be taking over this area, and we will have to move back west to remain in the British Zone... We are finding that some of the Russian DPs are showing some reluctance to return over the bridge, as they have heard rumours of the maltreatment of some of those who went over earlier and who it was thought had collaborated with the Nazi regime, and the Russian authorities had not been too particular in finding the right people, only acting on hearsay. Those who have been calling themselves Ukrainian citizens are also getting anxious. The Russian authorities consider this an offence, as they should be registering as Soviet citizens... We are still getting one or two Western nationals, who we put on a train for

Lüneberg where they are flown to Brussels... I was asked to take some sick people by ambulance to Lüneberg the other day, as they were unable to go on the train, making a round trip of over two hundred miles. The Austin ambulances are tiring to drive for long distances, but I was glad of the outing...

A lot more thinking is going on about the future of FAU work in NW Europe, we have all been sent a questionnaire to fill in, and there will be a meeting, to which every Section will send a representative, to discuss the findings and make a coherent plan. I have to say with the demobilisation of the older and more experienced members I cannot see how the present level of work can be continued. Maybe the number of Sections could be reduced with a reallocation of those members who are prepared to commit themselves to a further six months or so. I understand there are one or two older members returning to England from other overseas postings who would now like to work in Germany for a while, rather than take up their demobilisation at once, so this arrangement would also accommodate them and allow for their continued working under FAU auspices rather than having to join another voluntary body. For myself, as soon as my commitment under the National Service Act is over I would wish to come home, and get started in civil life, but that could be another 18 months away. I think I will probably have had enough by then, anyway. But the opinion of the older members seems to be that the FAU should be completely shut down, rather than struggle on with less experienced people, and maybe tarnish the past excellent record of the Unit. This doesn't seem to put too much trust in us younger members, but I have a feeling that it is this opinion which may well prevail. If so, the younger ones will have to transfer to other organisations, such as British Red Cross or Friends Relief Service, to work out our time under the National Service conditions. *[In the event the FAU Postwar Service was established, and quite a number returned to England to join it. I wanted to continue the work I was doing in Germany, so as will be seen, I transferred to the British Red Cross for my last year of service.]*

FAU, 205 Det. Mil. Gov., Rear HQ 30 Corps, BLA [Buxtehude, Germany], 2 July 1945

So sorry to hear about the damage to the pond *[in the garden of the family home in Welwyn Garden City]* by vandals. Just as it was doing so well. Has it upset the equilibrium of life in the pond? If you haven't got it sorted by the time I get home it will give me something to do. Strangely, in the garden of one of our billets, I came across a gnome fisherman identical to the one in Mummy's pond, but he had lost his fishing rod.

Gordon, the first on our list for home leave should have gone today, but no transport has come for him yet. I am third on the list. Yes, our team has remained unchanged since we entered Germany, but four are nearly due for demobilisation, so there will have to be changes soon. I don't know where the other FAU Sections are now, we only get news of them when Gerald visits us… Interested to hear the election is hotting up and that Daddy had been to a local election meeting. Any hope of the Labour candidate getting in? I am hoping that most people will come to see that only Labour has the radical ideas necessary to cope with the immense problems both at home and internationally. To go back to traditional Conservative policies, which failed so conspicuously in the 1930s, would be a missed opportunity, to say the least, but there will be many who will be sorry to see Churchill go after his leadership through the war. Not that Labour is without its dangers, but I believe there are enough men of a liberal bent in the party to prevent socialism going too far, and it will take at least the whole of a term of office to nationalise effectively the railways, mines, health service and so on, then the electorate will have time to reflect…

The changes to the areas of the Zones of Occupation of the Allies, which I mentioned before, has involved considerable movement of troops. We were withdrawn from Tangermünde when it became part of the Russian Zone, and are now situated at Buxtehude, north-west of Hamburg. Also 205 Det. has been attached to the 51st Highland Division HQ and will only be acting in an advisory capacity on DP and other Mil. Gov. matters from now on. Which really leaves us a bit superfluous – our forte is running things on the ground rather than advising. So I imagine we will be parting company with 205 soon. I think we will all be sorry to say goodbye as we have got to know many of the personnel and been through some exacting times together… Our work is bound to change anyway. Relief work, it seems to me, has three stages, emergency, interim and long term. The emergency is over, we are in the interim and fast approaching the longer term. The FAU teams have mostly been concerned with DPs, but the Western nationals and the Russians have mostly gone, and only Poles and Stateless are left. These people are being placed in more static camps, where they virtually run their own affairs, starting small businesses, like hairdressing and cobbling, starting allotments, and have their own church services and clinics. They are fed on German food rations. British Army officers supervise with occasional visits, but this could be an area of work for the FAU? *[See later developments, p.89]…* UNRRA is very slowly getting its act together. After the Rhine was crossed they said they would have 70 teams in the field in 3 to 4 weeks, three months later I doubt whether there are even a dozen. Second Army out of necessity, I suppose, have formed their own units to deal with DP matters. Mil. Gov. working through the local German authorities have control over civil life, and considering the size of the problem seem to be doing quite well. Schools and higher education are being restarted and in many towns a British Town Major has been installed, some are getting quite possessive of their areas, behaving a bit like the lord of the manor, which can be benevolent. If there is a future for the FAU in Germany it must in the longer term be in this area... Food could be a problem not necessarily this winter but beyond. Many farms are still deserted, and much of the livestock killed. Transport is very limited, the British Army has set up an organisation called 'Barleycorn' whereby Wehrmacht transport *[ex-German Army]* not involved with re-construction in bombed German cities, is being turned over to agricultural transport.

German soldiers are being released from PoW camps and put to work in organised groups on the land. German railways are slowly getting running again, but the rebuilding of bridges and railway lines is an immense task, and undamaged rolling stock and locomotives are scarce. Food will also be a problem in other European countries, particularly Holland, and maybe Belgium, but the Allied Governments are aware of the situation and trying to put plans into operation. If the FAU is to continue work in Germany the make up of the teams will have to change, with people coming in prepared to stay for a definite term and with concern for, and experience of work in the areas of education, health, youth clubs, local government and so on...

FAU, 205 Det. Mil. Gov., Rear HQ 30 Corps, BLA [Buxtehude], 7 July 1945

Great News! All being well I shall leave here on the 19th homeward bound! I shall be travelling with Roger, as they have modified the leave arrangements to allow two to be away from a Section at the same time. I don't know how long the journey will be, maybe two to three days. The train from Hamburg takes 6 hours to reach Ostend. Anyway here I come – all I shall want is a hot bath, a bed with clean sheets and my civvies. Pity we haven't a car, we are allowed 12 gals. of petrol on leave. Good to hear you have managed to mend the pond... I look forward to talking over with you both, while I am on leave, the options of what I might do when my time here is over. Things are not much clearer in my mind than when I came out...

Well, as I told you in my last letter, we moved out of Tangermünde just before the Russians were due to arrive. The Dutch liaison officer, who stayed behind to witness the handover has now rejoined the Det. and tells a rather grim story. The Polish and Czech officers who also stayed behind, at their own request, were taken away for interrogation and he never saw them again. He said the Red Army discipline, while giving the appearance of being draconian, in fact allowed the individual soldiers to behave in any way they liked towards the German people. The tobacco factory owner, with whom we had some dealings, was hanged in his own warehouse, and there was some looting and raping in the town... Since we arrived here we have had very little to do, although two or three of the team went to the 51st Highland Division HQ to discuss and advise on DP work in the area. As a result some of us are going on a fact finding exercise in the Division's five Brigade areas, which extend from Cuxhaven in the north to Hannover in the south, to discover the size of the problem. The findings will determine our work in the near future. The intention is to have all DPs home by the winter, apart from the Poles and the stateless for whom winter quarters will have to be found. See you soon!

I went on home leave for 10 days, but the next letter was written nearly a month later.

No 2 Relief Section FAU, att. 601 Mil. Gov. Det., BLA [Otterndorf], 8 August 1945

Here I am safe and sound back with the boys. Our return journey was a nightmare. After Freda and Daddy had left me at the station in London, John Freshwater turned up, he had also been on leave, so we travelled together. After a night at the transit camp at Purfleet we boarded an LST the next morning, setting sail almost at once, but some way on we turned back to Tilbury to pick up a trainload of troops. Then we anchored off Southend for several hours before making the crossing overnight, arriving at Ostend at 9.30am, but that day's train had already left. After a day and a night at the transit camp at Ostend we finally caught the train early the next morning. It crawled along all day but finally stopped at Bad Oyenhausen, where we were told it was not going any further, so we were obliged to get off the train and spent the rest of the night in a hotel for officers. The next day we had to search out some transport to take us to the British Red Cross HQ at Vlotho, as we had to find out whether our Section had moved and if so where it was now. In fact the Section had moved only a small way from its last location, so we caught a train around midnight for Hamburg arriving at 9 am. We contacted the FAU Section there and spent the night with them, and they kindly transported us to our Section at Otterndorf, about 15 miles east of Cuxhaven, the following day. Six days of travel! While at Ostend I met up with the first mixed FAU team to come to work in Germany. Deryck Moore, a very nice fellow known to Freda and John, was with the team. I was most amused as he was concerned over a staff car he was bringing over for Gerald to use, one of the woman members had insisted on driving it off the LST and had managed to knock off some valuable pieces!... Besides changing location our Section is no longer with 205 Det. and is operating on its own, apart for rations and mail which we get from 601 Mil. Gov. We are living in two empty flats and two German women come in and cook for us. There have also been some changes in personnel, George Champion has moved to another Section, Hugh Johns has gone to join a team who are tracing missing Red Cross parcels in France, work which has led him to some involvement with the black market in Paris! He expects to join a team in Austria soon. The three oldest team members, Len Darling, Harry Gaunt and Dennis Wickham are being demobbed in a fortnight. We shall miss them all, particularly Len who has been a good leader, guiding us through some difficult times. He is being replaced by Bill Barnes, lately returned from China, who is the son of Bishop Barnes of Birmingham. Because of his, and the others' imminent departure, Len is passing more responsibilities onto us younger ones. He has posted me part time to the 'city office' we have in the Rathaus *[town hall]* here. I only liaise, fill up forms and answer questions, but I feel important walking off every morning with a briefcase! ... Not much other news, but at least you now have my address to write to... Yes, Daddy, I think I can arrange to get the letter delivered to your German friend somehow... By the way the crossing was really smooth this time, but I was asleep most of the time.

No 2 Relief Section FAU, att. 601 Mil. Gov. (K) Det., BLA [Otterndorf], 15 August 1945

Although the expected news when it did come brought a great sense of relief that the war was finally over, the nature of the end was almost too much to bear. *[The news of the dropping of the atomic bombs and the end of the war with Japan.]* The local German people seem outwardly unaffected by it, but maybe it is because they have been through so much themselves and still have a lot to contend with... Weather very miserable, raining nearly all the time, and very windy off the sea. It is just under a mile to the coast, the country crossed with numerable narrow waterways, rather pretty and always so clean. The other evening, after the rain had stopped, I and some others went for a walk towards the sea, and came across a navigable creek with a number of fishing boats tied up.

We got into conversation with an 'old salt', he wore the traditional heavy navy blue jersey, and rough, orangy-brown trousers, a peaked cap, and wooden clogs. Yes, he was smoking a pipe, but he wasn't splicing a rope. He appeared to talk two types of German. The first, rough and guttural, almost like Dutch *[could it have been Plattdeutsch?]*, and we could barely understand a word, he then switched to normal German, which I felt didn't come quite so naturally to him. He was very friendly and pleased to talk, we went on board and he described all the parts of the boat in English, names we gathered he had picked up from English fishing boats before the war, while fishing in the North Sea and calling in on British ports. During the war, although fishing in the North Sea was not usually possible, he had sailed in the Baltic, going through the Kiel Canal I suppose, and had visited places in Denmark, Norway, Sweden and even Finland. There seems to be a number of fishing boats around here and there is a fish market in Cuxhaven... There is not a great deal for us to do here, but we are going around collecting the odd DP family still on farms and have even found a patient who had been left behind in hospital. We take them to the nearest appropriate camp for repatriation. But we are coming across far more personal problems now. Some of the families are happily settled and don't wish to move anywhere, let alone back to their country of origin, but there is pressure from governments for their nationals to be repatriated, and the attitude of the British and German authorities in such cases has not yet been made clear. We intend to leave them where they are until told otherwise as they obviously get on with the local German people. Then there are cases where a DP has married a German, if the DP is made to return home can the German partner go as well, or even want to, as some Governments are not recognising such marriages as legal. Then there can be financial problems. One man had 2,000 marks in a German bank, but couldn't withdraw it as he was in the British Zone and it had been paid into a bank now in the Russian Sector. That could take a very long time to sort out. Problems of property, like the man who now owned some horses and cattle and wanted to take them home with him to Yugoslavia, he was finally obliged to sell them, but then found he couldn't take the money out of the country as it was considered too large a sum. I expect there are many such cases elsewhere, but these are ones we have come across in our small area. We can do little more than put the individuals in touch with other authorities and sometimes provide transport for this. Some of the complications which are caused when you forcibly move large numbers of people!

Two cinemas and a small theatre have now opened in Cuxhaven, so we have somewhere to go in an evening. We went to an ENSA *[British*

Services Entertainment Agency] show last week. The most popular feature seemed to be the 'sing alongs', the whole place resounding to renderings of 'Pistol Packin' Mamma' and the 'White Cliffs of Dover', and as the majority of the audience was from the 51st Highland Division, 'Loch Lomond'... Further to our conversation while I was home on leave about my future, and as I seem to have spare time at the moment, I wonder if you know of a book or two about the silversmith business, traditions, history, as well as technical, which might help me to decide whether to take the Edward Barnard & Sons idea any further *[the family silversmith business in London which it was considered I might join]*... The Section continues to change, Len, Colin and Dennis are due to leave very soon, and two new boys have arrived as well as the new leader, Bill Barnes. In a strange way we are more together now we have left 205, having to do some cooking, washing up and similar chores ourselves, I rather welcome that. We had our old 205 Major to dinner the other evening and he remarked how he missed us and our chatter from the officer's mess... The realisation that the war has at last ended is sinking in, but also the fact that the world has now got to learn to live with the atomic bomb. The arrival of nuclear energy brings tremendous possibilities for good and evil, but I have the feeling that politics have not kept pace with science. We now need some form of World Federation more than ever, and an understanding between USA and USSR has become imperative. Rocket science brings the possibility of space travel just round the corner. H.G. Wells doesn't look so far fetched now!

No 2 Relief Section, FAU, att. 601 Mil. Gov. Det., BLA [Otterndorf], 18 August 1945

I'm sending this to Almeley *[Herefordshire]*, as I think you will still be there. I hope you are having good weather, it's been really wet here recently. There is little work for us here, and Major Sharp of 205, who visited us recently, said it is scandalous that such expertise as ours should not be in use, he was always rather keen on us! Anyway he has found us a job, preparing a camp as winter quarters for Polish DPs. It is an area we know well around Harpstedt and we shall be moving next week... I went to a German film the other evening, one gets in for 3d or 6d!

I was able to follow the story, but most of the dialogue was too quick for me. The technique, if that's the word, is rather different to British and American films, and rather more modest than what we have come to expect from Hollywood. It was called 'A Night in Venice', but I didn't get the names of the actors...

British Policy in Occupied Germany

In view of the references in my letters to official policy in the British Zone of Germany I thought it would be of interest to include here some extracts from the text of an important talk on radio by Field Marshal Montgomery, Commander-in-Chief of the British occupation forces to the German people, on 6 August 1945. It is of considerable historical importance as it shows the tolerant British Government attitude to the German people that prevailed only three months after a desperate war for survival. The enlightened approach led to the establishment of a democracy in at least Western Germany, and contrasted so remarkably with the policy after the First World War of 'squeezing them until the pips squeak', which had led, inevitably, to hyper-inflation, vast unemployment, the destruction of the economy, and created a situation where to many German people the ideas of the Nazi Party seemed a way out of their difficulties.

In his broadcast Montgomery said:

The first stage in the rehabilitation of Germany is under way. I am now going to proceed with the second stage of Allied policy. In this stage it is my intention that you shall have freedom to get down to your own way of life subject only to the provisions of military security and necessity... we want to give you an objective and hope for the future.

I will relax by stages the present restrictions on the freedom of the press. It is Allied policy ... to encourage in Germany the formation of free trade unions and democratic political parties which may form the basis of an ordered and peaceful German society in the future.

We aim at the restoration of local self-government throughout Germany on democratic principles... It is our purpose also to reorganise the judicial system in accordance with the principles of democracy, of justice under the law, and of equal rights for all citizens without distinction of race.

You may hold public meetings and discussions. I am anxious that you should talk over your problems among yourselves and generally set on foot measures to help yourselves. Your children are at present lacking juvenile organisations and facilities for education, and to encourage the forming of such organisations on a voluntary basis for religious, cultural, health and recreational activities, educational facilities will be provided at a relatively early date.

I have relaxed the rules about fraternisation. This will enable us to have contact with you and to understand your problems more easily. The coming winter will be a difficult time, there is much to mend and put right and time is short. We are faced with the probability of a shortage of food and coal, insufficient accommodation, and inadequate services of transportation and distribution. It is well that you should realise this now.

I will do all I can to get the population of the British Zone through the coming winter, but you, the German people, must work to help yourselves. I will continue to see that you are all kept informed by radio and newspapers of how we are progressing. I will give you German news as well as foreign news. I expect the co-operation of you all in the second stage of the Allied policy.

6. Dünsen

August to December 1945

No 2 Relief Section, FAU, c/o 205 Det. Mil. Gov., HQ 30 Corps, BAOR [British Army of the Rhine; Dünsen, near Harpstedt, Germany], 31 August 1945

Please note change of address, we are back with 205 for the time being, actually we are some seven miles away, although in their area, and are attached only for rations, mail, etc., although it was Major Sharp who wanted us for this present job. Also BLA (British Liberation Army) has been dropped and replaced with BAOR (British Army of the Rhine). We moved here some days ago, near the little village of Dünsen, some 20 miles south of Bremen, we were in the area about four months ago, it's strange to come back now it's all so peaceful. We are in a large forested area with many brick and wooden buildings dotted about, which was a German Army camp, but disturbingly it was surrounded by a minefield, which has only just been finally cleared. We hope they have done a good job!

We had to start by organising parties of German workers who were brought in to clear and clean the buildings, and lay on the electricity and water, etc. The surrounding land has been cleared of all the debris of war, what a mess had been left behind. Now we can start getting it ready for a possible couple of thousand people, who may start arriving in a few days. Organising food supplies, ensuring there are medical and central feeding facilities. Finding a suitable building for a school, there could be up to 200 children, and we have been told the community will want to have places for a cinema, drama, dances, concerts, but the Poles will run all these activities themselves. There is a field not far away where football can be played, but we are very short of sports equipment. At the moment it looks as though we could be here all winter – anyway we have found two very nice houses for ourselves *[see photo overleaf]*, although they took some cleaning up. We have two German women who live in and cook for us. Arthur Jewson, who has always seen to the catering side of the Section, found them, they are from a part of Germany now occupied by the Russians and have no intention of going back. Well that's enough, it's well past 11.30 pm and there is hardly any electric light – at least you now know I'm well and working again.

2 Relief Section FAU, c/o 205 Mil. Gov. Det., HQ 30 Corps, BAOR [Dünsen], 2 September 1945

Just received several of your letters together, taking 14 days to get here. Hope you have been getting mine. Glad to hear about your time in Almeley with mostly good weather. That was a jolly good walk, Daddy, I should have been proud of that. The best I have done was in the Lake District with Anthony Harris, we did two peaks over 2,000ft and then Great Gable, about 3,000ft, about 18 miles in the day… Everything in the camp is progressing, and we have had a few arrivals. I forgot to say, when we were clearing up one of the buildings we found in the cellar a cat and three kittens, they didn't look in too good a condition and must have been finding their own food, as there hasn't been anybody here as far as we know since the soldiers who cleared the minefield. The kittens couldn't have been much over a week old so we took them to our house and are feeding them up. Just like the hospital at Bangour in Scotland,

Billet at Dünsen Camp

kittens everywhere, fluffy balls of mischief. While walking with Roger in the area one evening we came across some really large rats, we had heard a hissing noise and saw one rat quite transfixed by a small snake seemingly unable to move. I'm sure the rat was big enough to have eaten the snake in one bite, but it seemed petrified. At the noise of our approach the snake slithered away and the rat seemed to come to and then ran off. Extraordinary. We have seen one or two of these snakes around, quite small ones but I have no idea what they are, but we give them a wide berth just in case they are poisonous…

2 Relief Section, FAU, 205 Mil. Gov. Det., HQ 30 Corps, BAOR [Dünsen], 9 September 1945

In answer to your question the food shortage in Germany does not affect us personally, as we are fed on Army rations, brought in from Britain, America and Canada, about the only local produce we use is apples. We have ample rations, in fact we don't draw out all we are entitled to, and have enough to feed the two German women who work for us, although it is strictly forbidden to give army rations to German civilians. Of course, we do feel it living so adequately ourselves while just outside our door there are people suffering severe shortages, but this presumably must be what most aid workers have to learn to live with. The Army medical services are good, although spread over large areas, but we always have our own ambulances to take us anywhere, fortunately we haven't had the need to test this! There is really no need to worry about me. I'm sure I eat better than you do at home. The food situation for the German people is looking grimmer. Although things are being done, we understand, for example that Canadian wheat is being brought in to Hamburg.

We have around 1,500 Poles in the camp now, although it is more like running a self-contained estate. A whole community is getting going – the Poles have established for themselves a school, which has classes for adults in the evening, a church and Sunday school, nursery school, some rooms which are a clinic and mini-hospital. Pigs and poultry are being kept and allotments started. A rudimentary police force and fire brigade are in training. There is a laundry and a large central kitchen which provides meals. Also a large hall which acts as a cinema, theatre or dance hall, as required. The Poles have their own way of doing things, so we have to be diplomatic, but they are very cooperative, energetic and inventive. But it was hard work to get it started. Many of the buildings were in a state of disrepair, and we had to get groups of German workers in to lay on water, electricity and sewage again. We had to find much of the materials and tools with our very limited transport, and a hundred and one authorities to negotiate with – British, American and German. To ensure coal and wood fuel supplies for the coming winter, and regularise the supply of food. Check that arrangements were being made for the payment, from local German authorities, of the German workers and all the supplies, endless red tape to go through.

The other evening we went to the opening dance of the Dünsen Camp Entertainment Committee, we had a formal written invitation. On our arrival the music stopped, the floor cleared and we walked across the room to be met in the middle by the Polish Major who is the Camp Commandant, and his officers, who all saluted, clicked heels and shook hands. We were then conducted to a corner which had been marked off with bushes in tubs, where had they got it all from? The major delivered a welcome speech in good English, and then sat down at little tables, drank very poor coffee and smoked cigarettes. We were offered some very dubious looking 'vodka' which we all politely declined, in some camps we had heard of a spirit being made from potatoes. Dancing started up again and obviously picked girls hovered near at hand should we wish to dance. The band were not bad, but the dancing was rather different from the foxtrots and waltzes we are used to. The dances are all mixed into one without breaks and it is repeated over and over again, utterly exhausting. Maybe that was the only tune the band could play? At one stage we were entertained by six girls and six men in high boots doing some Polish equivalent of 'cossack' dancing. I have seen better, but it was none the less very rousing, stamping boots on the floor, tambourines and castanettes, wild drumming and a piano accordion, and in the heat of the dance wild yells! We were amazed at what they could come up with in two or three weeks.

2 Relief Section, FAU, 205 Det. Mil. Gov., HQ 30 Corps, BAOR [Dünsen], 15 September 1945

David goes on leave this week, and he said he would be willing to collect my mended watch from Gordon Square *[FAU HQ in London]* on his way back. If you could kindly label the package with my name and address to be collected by David Curtis and leave it in the Overseas Office, where we collect passports, it should be alright. Very many thanks. David is taking his second home leave, he is the only one left of the original team who landed on the beaches in France – Len, Colin and Dennis have all been demobbed. There are ten in the team now, average age around 22, Bill the new leader is 26 and Arthur 28, but he is staying by choice.

We had an inspection by a Brigadier from HQ who said he was very favourably impressed with the standard in the camp. So Bill took the opportunity to explain our difficulties in finding equipment. That very same evening we had a delivery of almost everything we were looking for, and another delivery later! We are now officially called a Polish Community Camp. Yes, we only have Poles in the camp. Most other DPs have left Germany now, including the Russians, the Westerners have long gone. Which now leaves only Italians, who are starting to be repatriated, and Yugoslavs and Greeks and, of course the so called Stateless – Lithuanians, Latvians and Estonians. The Poles are now by far the largest group, but there is talk that the Allies would like to get those who lived west of the Curzon Line to return by the end of the year. East of the Curzon Line has now mostly become part of Russia, but even that part of Poland west of the line is still occupied by Russian troops, although ostensibly governed by Communist Poles sympathetic to Russia. So it is a bit 'pie in the sky' to think that any Polish DPs now in Germany will agree to return there. *[Curzon Line: the eastern frontier of Poland, proposed by Lord Curzon and recognised by the Allies in 1919 but not actually adopted. However it became a virtual reality in 1945, having been accepted as the basis for the future demarcation at the Teheran Conference in 1943 by Russia, Great Britain and the USA.]*

It is difficult to comprehend but we have heard that the Zones of Occupation will be made 'open', so that people will be free to go where they wish. *[In fact this did not happen, although German refugees from eastern parts of Germany and those expelled from the areas given to Poland were allowed into the western zones.]* In readiness for the floods of Germans from the Eastern parts, transit camps are being established in the British Zone. It has been suggested that the FAU may be able to help with these. They will be important as a check on the spread of disease, as the British Zone is fairly epidemic free at the moment and a programme of mass inoculations are being carried out... I suppose one should not spread unconfirmed rumours, but what we have heard many about conditions in the Russian Zone and are alarming, if true. No food rationing system exists, people just get what they can, how they can. Local government hardly exists. The factories are being stripped of all machinery and equipment, even down to the telephone wires along the roads, and shipped back to Russia.

No 2 Relief Section, FAU, 205 Det. Mil. Gov., HQ 30 Corps, BAOR [Dünsen], 19 September 1945

We are endeavouring to carry out a complete registration of everyone in the camp in connection with repatriation, but it is very unlikely that any will wish to return to their homeland. We have heard nothing more of the idea of camps for German refugees from the East… Gerald Gardiner is going home soon and his place is being taken by Michael Rowntree, late of the Hadfield-Spears unit, who operated in North Africa and Southern Europe. Now that we have our own house I find the evenings free to do more reading. Could you look through the shelves in my bedroom and send any books on History and German?

2 Relief Section, FAU, 205 Det. Mil. Gov., HQ 30 Corps, BAOR [Dünsen], 23 September 1945

Work in the camp goes on apace. A few more buildings have been cleaned and put into use, to increase our capacity, but we also had to condemn one or two of the wooden buildings which were beyond repair and are having them pulled down to make firewood for the winter. We have been asked to increase our efforts to gather in all Polish nationals who may still be in isolated places in our area… Probably owing to the increased numbers the sewage system broke down, and work parties have had to be organised to dig up the drains in various parts of the camp and lay more pipes. I have been trying to draw a large map to show where the pipes run, but a lot of it has to be guess work…

We are rather isolated here being the only British unit for some miles around, and some of the local people have come to look upon us as the appropriate administration to sort out their problems. The other day a Greek doctor, who had lived in Germany for many years, thought because he was an Allied national he should be made the Director of the local hospital instead of the current occupant who was German, and was most put out that we couldn't effect the change! We keep in touch with the local Bürgermeisters , and were able to suggest to one that some workers from a brewery, the only factory that seemed to be working, might be better employed getting some of the deserted farms back in operation, which is priority at the moment. There is a real shortage of German male workers, due I suppose to the massive casualties during the war and the hundreds of thousands of prisoners held in Russia and elsewhere…

Autumn is approaching, the leaves are turning brown and the floor of the forest is littered with pine needles, reminding me a little of Scotland last year which was particularly beautiful. I love all the seasons in turn but I am especially fond of autumn, the golden browns and the dark greens of the conifers, even the half-mists which drift close to the ground. It is getting colder now, but following our experience in the Ardennes, we shan't mind the winter half as much this time, as we won't have to move every so often and have a house to return to, which we can make quite cosy… In answer to your questions, Len Darling left us before we came here, and is working pro-tem in Gordon Square *[FAU HQ]* waiting to be released. He was so keen to get back to England as he has a wife and baby, and wants to take up teacher training. Michael Frankton went to France, I believe, and I haven't seen Giles Cooper since the Antwerp days. Gaydu in his last letter said he was now a full Lieutenant, but complained that he had very little to do, although he was fearing he may be sent to the Far East. Reg is on a mechanics course in Leeds, he volunteered for China, but changed his mind and has now put in for a driving job in France. David Grensted wrote a long letter, now doing TB nursing in Scotland, but the letter developed into a long religious discourse, which was hard to follow, I find him so serious and needs to lighten up. Gerald Gardiner is resigning, he can, of course, leave whenever he likes, as a barrister and over military age he was not called up, and joined the FAU of his own free will, leaving a very prosperous practice to do so…

2 Relief Section, FAU, 205 Det. Mil. Gov., HQ 30 Corps, BAOR [Dünsen], 2 October 1945

In answer to your question, Bill Barnes is a very capable fellow, not at all the same as Len Darling, he makes a good Section Leader, but different. He has spent most of his Unit time in China and India, slightly short tempered, but still suffers from the effects of malaria, which may be a reason… Yes, I do see your point about bartering with cigarettes, but with currency virtually useless the locals would rather have cigs. or soap, as they know they are sure to be able to buy bread and other essentials with them. We are simply doing them a good turn. There is an interesting article in Issue 74 of the *FAU Chronicle* by Ham Mills on 'Conchies at the Front' reflecting on how we have to be aware when working so closely with soldiers in often difficult and dangerous circumstances to try not be influenced by their attitudes to such things as small scale looting and so on, and stay neutral to their views.

We received a letter from Corps HQ reminding us that now was the time to put in for our 'France and Germany Campaign' ribbons. All those who served six months or more while the war was on are eligible, which applies to those in FAU Sections 1 and 2 who landed on the beaches in France last September. We, of course, only came across at the end of December and as the war ended in May, we just missed the deadline. In any case, those members who were eligible decided to decline the offer and wrote a polite letter, explaining that it would be hypocritical for them to accept and thereby celebrate a military victory. Although they saw that in a way it was a recognition of their work done in conflict situations, unlike that of UNRRA and other voluntary bodies, who have come out since, and whose work is being done after the fighting ceased, very valuable as it is.

We have been advised to undertake a Typhus inoculation campaign, and supplies of vaccine have been delivered. We have had notices put up throughout the camp in Polish, saying how dangerous Typhus is and to come and get inoculated. A room was set aside and we spent all day from 9 to 5 doing injections, under the supervision of a Polish doctor, with John *[Tanner]*, who is a medical student, claiming he had done over a hundred.

With the work having settled into more of a routine we are taking Sundays off, listening to the wireless or reading in an easy chair. On Sunday John read from the Bible at breakfast, Bill started digging in the garden, Martin learning Greek in an armchair, Roger playing football with some Poles, and now as the weather is getting colder, Gordon and I decided to try and light the two stoves in the cellars which heat the water and the radiators, so we can all have hot baths when we wish. The trouble may be fuel, we have coke for about six weeks, but from where do we get more? There are plenty of fallen branches in the forest, but it would need a lot of collecting. We all gather for a cup of tea in the evening before going to bed in the sitting room and talk over the day's happenings. It is all rather comfortable and I wouldn't mind seeing the winter through here…

2 Relief Section FAU, 205 Det. Mil. Gov., HQ 30 Corps, BAOR [Dünsen], 5 October 1945

I only wrote three days ago, but I learned tonight that John Ford has died. He was in the Scots Guards stationed in the Ruhr, he developed pneumonia with spinal complications.

John you may remember was at school with me, and I brought him home on one occasion, a large lad, we did quite a bit of cross-country running together. Roger heard the news from his parents who also live in Barnet and know John's parents well. John's mother and sister, Janet, were flown out and visited him in a military hospital in Cologne. Roger and I will write to them. I met Janet at the last Chris reunion I went to, but John was already in the army… About my raincoats, I have to confess I had forgotten I had three! By all means let John have one, and Daddy the new one without a belt, I don't like the thought of him having to squeeze into my old worn out one, while the other hangs unused in the cupboard. I don't want any coupons for them now, but the situation may be different by the time I get home…

2 Relief Section, FAU, 205 Det. Mil. Gov., HQ 30 Corps, BAOR [Dünsen], 9 October 1945

Many thanks for the three parcels, enclosing books and things, they came really quickly. I do hope I'm not being too much trouble. David returned from leave on Saturday and brought my watch which he had collected from Gordon Square, thank you very much for seeing to that, it seems to be working very nicely. David seemed a bit concerned about the food situation in England, what is it like? I wish I could share my rations with you – fish for breakfast and often meat twice a day, and as much tinned cheese as we like. We are also feeding two German women, who cook and clean for us, and their two children (four and five) from our rations and don't notice it. They joined us at Otterndorf and were delighted to get the work for their keep, and were willing to move with us when we came here. I'm not sure of their story, but they were the wives of Wehrmacht soldiers, and were living under very difficult conditions with relatives. One of them, Charlotte, is rather keen on Arthur Jewson, who undertakes the catering side of the Section. *[Later they went to England and got married. The last I heard, many years ago now, they were living in Newcastle.]*

The camp is running quite smoothly, although we always have to be ready for the unexpected. For example, the daily milk delivery was suddenly halved, and our office was besieged by irate mothers and their children demanding more. The situation was temporarily eased by dipping into our stocks of tinned milk, and trying to explain the situation to them. Some camps we understand have had quite serious food riots, where it was thought that local German farmers were feeding better than the DPs. It is difficult for Mil. Gov. to discover if farmers are holding back some of their produce for themselves. Many of the DPs feel they should be getting whatever is available, not the Germans who have made them suffer. The fact is that it is only those Germans living in the country who may be benefiting in this way, those in the cities are much worse off. Bill has decided to start a weekly 'current affairs' talk with all the 'block leaders' and other camp officials to explain the realities of the food and supplies situation and what Mil. Gov. is trying to do about it, hoping that the more level headed ones will be able to reason with the disaffected elements.

There are now several parties of Poles active in the forest felling trees for winter fuel. I went up to see how things were getting on. I found my way to the heart of the forest, where I could hear the quiet being broken by the sound of saws and axes, and shouts of 'timber' in Polish as another tall fir crashed to the ground. Swarms of men then started sawing and chopping and in no time piles of logs were being stacked up. There was a lovely pine smell in the air and I could have watched this hive of activity for ages, but I also felt a little sad to see so many trees being cut down, although realising that it was to meet a very real need. One of the German Forest wardens told us that in the past the trees were regularly cut down for pit props anyway. Also in the forest there are several ammunition dumps, some in bunkers underground. The Army is busy removing bombs and shells and taking them some two miles away where they have a place for conducting controlled explosions. Several times a day there is a terrific noise as another lot goes up. They say it will go on for months so you can imagine what a large arsenal it is. I'm glad to see the stuff being got rid of, but I wish there was a quieter way – it makes you jump out of your skin!... We have heard that the arrangements with the Russians for repatriating Poles and other Eastern DPs has broken down, mainly because they say they cannot provide the necessary shelter, food or transport. Which sounds a bit of an excuse. Anyway FAU Section 6 is being allowed into the Russian Zone and is setting up a transit camp for them north of Berlin. If the USSR can't do it the FAU can! It is rather remarkable that the Russians have allowed a British unit into their zone, and then that the FAU rather than UNRRA were chosen for the job.

2 Section FAU, c/o HQ 51st Div., BAOR [Dünsen], 18 October 1945

We have been having our booster injections, TABT in one arm and Typhus in the other, I'm not usually affected, but I have had stiff arms, a headache and felt slightly groggy, but o.k. now... Please note slight change in address, its simply a new postal system which has come into operation and means we have lost our connection with '205' and also have to collect our rations from the new venue... We have realised that the narrow lane which runs for about 3 miles from the camp to the road could clearly get snowed up. So we are indenting for a week's rations to have as a standby, and have set some Poles to making sledges!... We were invited to a Polish concert in the camp last Sunday. A mixed choir sang folk songs intermixed with prose and poetry. The singing was good but we didn't understand a word. It ended with a stirring rendition of the Polish national anthem, the pianist following this by thumping out, not too convincingly, 'God save the King'. As guests in the front row we felt we should get to our feet, but no sooner had we done so than the playing stopped, as he didn't know any more! However, everyone cheered, and the Polish major came over and shook our hands. I think the Poles are rather class conscious. Most of the officers have rooms to themselves in set aside buildings, yet in the rest of the camp there are two if not three families to a room. We tried, diplomatically, to rearrange things but both parties were shocked at our proposals, the 'working class' families wouldn't dream of asking the officers to move... Len Darling has left the Unit as he was able to move to a job in Social Services. Reg has transferred to IGCR *[Inter-governmental Committee for Refugees]* as a driver, but will be working mainly in the American Zone... Under our UK leave arrangements I should be due for some around Christmas. The Army leave scheme has stalled because of the congestion in the transit camps and shortage of ships, some are said to be waiting in ports to unload, and NAAFI supplies are also getting held up so they have had to reduce what they can make available, but I expect it is only a temporary hitch.

No 2 Relief Section, FAU, c/o HQ 51st (H) Div., BAOR [Dünsen], 28 October 1945

Bill and I are due for a 72 hours leave, so we have decided to spend it travelling in the south, maybe as far as Oberstdorf on the Swiss border, but we shall have to get a pass to enter the American Zone, and possibly the French Zone. Maybe we could go to Munich, so if you could let me have your friend's address there, the one you and Freda stayed with in Easter 1938, a visit may be possible. What do you think?... The past week we have been preparing to receive a further 350 Poles, who have been living in outlying places, farm barns and the like, which would not be suitable for the winter. This has meant obtaining extra supplies and so on. In answer to Mummy's questions, the majority of the Poles live in brick buildings, formerly army barracks, officer's houses, stores and offices, which are scattered round the edges of the forest. Many of the buildings, although structurally sound, had some internal damage, doors, windows, etc., and we had parties of German labour to do repairs, lay on the electricity and water before the Poles arrived. There are also many wooden buildings, some of which we have had pulled down as too dilapidated, and one or two recently constructed Nissen huts put up by the Royal Engineers. The difficulty here is the shortage of stoves for heating and electrical equipment, such as cable, bulbs and switches. But this is only to be expected as the only source of supply is German, and there can't be many factories making these things yet. There is a school and a church in the camp, both housed in wooden buildings, not totally suitable, but adequate. The church is, of course, Roman Catholic, run by an ex-PoW Polish Army padre. The vast majority of the Poles are Roman Catholic, there are one or two Orthodox, but they have no priest and have expressed no wish to have a church. There are at least two Polish Jews, who survived concentration camps. The RC padre is very active, taking classes in the school and the Sunday school and trying to form a Boy Scout Troop.

Yes, it is a real forest, but interspersed with plantations of pine, there are many squirrels and birds, and we have even had glimpses of deer, but they are very timid. There can't be many, I would have thought they would have long gone, with the shortage of food, and the mines... Several severe gales recently with trees blown over. I hear on the wireless you have been having the same... You'll be pleased to know we have had a new clothes issue and I have received a pair of pyjamas, woolly gloves, a shirt, and a new battle dress, and a leather jerkin to come...

The Unit held a conference at the British Red Cross HQ at Vlotho, where future policy for the teams in North-West Europe was considered. It has been decided to send another FAU team into the Russian Zone to help with the repatriation of Polish and other eastern DPs, and five FAU teams are to be transferred to the Ruhr where it is felt the need is now the greatest. There was terrible destruction there from bombing during the war, and very few factories are operating yet, due partly because little coal is being mined to power them. We understand that many places are not receiving the proper food ration as transport is so poor, and there are still many homeless. It is clear that Mil. Gov. really wants to help the German people through the winter, but the task is daunting in all respects. *[See Field Marshall Montgomery's radio talk on pp.87–88]* This is the first sign of FAU policy moving away from caring for DPs to work with the German population. Apparently UNRRA have taken over DP work in 8 Corps district and will be doing so in our 30 Corps area soon, so we maybe on the move after all, which would be goodbye to our hoped for cosy winter here. Well we didn't come out here for a holiday!

No 2 Section FAU, c/o HQ 51st (H) Div., BAOR [Dünsen], 6 November 1945

Sorry for not writing for some days, but Bill and I finally got away on our leave, for four days. What we originally planned to do turned out to be wildly optimistic, if you remember we had hoped to reach the Swiss border, but we didn't even get to Munich. After looking more closely at the distances involved and the petrol we would have available, we had to take with us all we needed in jerry cans, together with our rations, water, etc., it became obvious we would have to be more conservative.

So in the event I was unable to visit your friends there, however as the civilian mail is working again I have put your letter in the post. I wrote my address on the back and if it is not delivered it will be returned to me. Nevertheless we got quite a way and had a most interesting time. We left early on the Friday morning travelling south through Hannover and Hameln (of Pied Piper fame) and went on to Kassel, entering the American Zone without seeing anyone at all at the crossing point. We parked our Austin ambulance in a wood and slept the night warmly and comfortably in the back on the stretchers. Set off again early, after shaving with cold water in the frosty air and headed towards Eisenach. However, just before the town we ran into a road barrier preventing us from entering the Russian Zone, and the rather stern faced guards made clear we couldn't go any further. So reluctantly we retraced our steps, before turning south-west through Fulda and on the road to Würzburg, before turning off to spend the night in the ambulance about 900ft up with a perfect view over Brückenau.

The next day we headed west over the river Main and through mountain scenery to Aschaffenburg and Frankfurt. Then on to Wiesbaden to Rüdersheim on the Rhine, from there we followed the winding road alongside the river, past the Lorelei rock and into the French Zone. Here we were stopped and questioned, but the French soldiers were very friendly and seemed to want to simply chat, rather than enquire what we were up to, and even invited us to join them in a drink. We thought it probably advisable to decline as it was already late. Bill's fluent French came in handy. Again we turned off to find a quiet spot to spend the night as before.

The last day we crossed the Rhine at Koblenz still in the French Zone, but soon entered the American Zone and passed through Remagen *[made famous in the war by the bridge episode and subsequent film]* to Bad Godesberg, Bonn and Cologne, where we stopped to see the cathedral, still standing, but all around quite flat. Recrossed the Rhine into the Ruhr, where the destruction beggared belief, passing through Wuppertal, Bochum, Münster and Osnabrück and so home arriving about 10pm. Bill was very happy for me to do the driving, about 800 miles! I will tell you more when I get home – sunset over the Rhine, mountain roads, hills, forests and lovely old towns and villages - which may not be all that long as second home leave allocations have come through. At the moment I am down for mid-December, which could mean I should be home over Christmas, barring any unexpected happenings. But whatever do I do for presents, there is nothing in the shops, maybe a bar of soap from NAAFI !

No 2 Section FAU, c/o HQ 51st Div., BAOR [Dünsen Camp], 13 November 1945

Last night I was officer on duty, reading alone, when one of the Polish camp guards knocked on the door to say he had found two suspicious German women roaming around the camp. The camp is forbidden to all Germans and it was well after curfew time so it became a security matter. The women were very reluctant to talk but it appeared they were from Bremen, which is 25 kilometres away, but I couldn't discover how they had travelled and why they were here. So I decided to call in the military police, who took them away, remarking they were probably just 'common women' looking for 'business'. We didn't hear any more.

I found the report of the discussion in the House about the releasing of 'conchies' from their conditions most interesting. See Hansard in *The Times* of the 10th and small column on back page of the *News Chronicle* also the 10th. The arrangement already announced is that conchies would be released after the last person in their equivalent group in the Army had gone, which would probably be about 4 to 6 weeks later. But apparently many MPs from all parts of the House spoke in favour of exempting members of the FAU from this, saying they should be released at the same time. Especially outspoken was an Army Major who while serving had seen the Unit at work in dangerous situations. You never can tell! We'll just have to wait and see. It still has to have its third reading and get through the Lords. Although it is more than possible the FAU would not wish to be made an exemption.

The past week we have been settling in another 300 or so Poles, but some of the blocks are getting a bit crowded, so we found another place about 2 miles away in Harpstedt. It was an old Arbeitsdienst camp, but in rather an awful state and the water wasn't drinkable. However, we appealed to Mil. Gov. who put us in touch with 173 Pioneer Company, who did the necessary work and agreed, as they were stationed so near, to take over the running of the camp if they could call on us if necessary. There was an Australian Lieutenant in charge who seemed rather diffident at the prospect, but I think we managed to put him in the picture and ease his doubts.

Our vehicles are beginning to show wear and tear, and one truck has had to go into REME *[Royal Electrical and Mechanical Engineers]* for a complete overhaul. On appealing to Mil. Gov. they provided us with a German private car, which we suppose was requisitioned. We were a bit dubious about this, but realised that even if the German owners still existed they wouldn't be able to use it without petrol. We intend to return it the moment the emergency is over and it is in a good cause. We do already have a car bequeathed to us when we took over from the Americans at Hesslingen, that was of course rather a different situation. We understand that the few Volkswagen cars now beginning to come off the production line are being allocated to the Army and the Red Cross have had some.

No 2 Section FAU, c/o HQ 51st Div., BAOR [Dünsen], 25 November 1945

Interested to hear that Winifred White *[I believe she was on the staff of the Quaker weekly The Friend]* would like to print some extracts from my letters. I don't think I'm very keen on that. Anyway the FAU are rather strict on members writing to the press, and I think she would have to clear anything she wanted to include with Gordon Square *[FAU HQ]* first. I think Robin Whitworth is the man to see.

We are still getting a few Poles away, from those groups who have finally expressed a wish to be repatriated, but it will have to cease soon as the land route is to be closed and going by sea will not be possible when the Baltic Sea freezes. So they will then have to wait until the spring. It had been reckoned that nearly 80% wanted to go, but in fact only some 25% have actually gone; apart from the travel difficulties, the Poles themselves keep changing their minds as differing rumours of how things are in Poland keep coming through. So plans have now got to be put in place to provide food, fuel and clothing for much larger numbers than had been expected, making Dünsen the largest Assembly centre in this area. We are only one of two Relief teams in 30 Corps area and Major Sharp (now acting Lt. Col.) doesn't want to lose us and has told Corps HQ he can't possibly do without us. But it is policy now to get UNNRA teams to take over DP work and Red Cross and COBSRA teams to concentrate on the German population. It will be interesting to see who will prevail. Although our personal inclinations are that the situation now requires us to leave DPs and move onto to work with the German people.

No 2 Section, FAU, c/o HQ 51st Div., BAOR [Dünsen], 2 December 1945

Just a short note. I leave here on the 13th for home, so expect me soon after. I won't be writing again. Much the same here, except that we now have a new 3-tonner and 15 cwt truck, which is a great help. George Champion, who moved to another Section when the war ended, paid us a visit and brought copies of the photographs he had taken earlier *[see Chapter 2]*; one when we were in the chateau in Belgium and one in Germany where our convoy is halted under a road sign indicating 27 kms to Bremen, which was still in German hands at the time. How he managed to have a camera and film I don't know, we were asked not to bring cameras with us when we first came out.

There is a gap of over four weeks until the next letter.

7. Hannover

January to July 1946

No 2 Section, FAU, c/o HQ 51st Div., BAOR [Dünsen], 3 January 1946

Just a line to let you know I'm back with the Section again. Quite a quick and easy journey.

I met the others at Liverpool Street station and we travelled together to Harwich where we embarked on a large boat the *Duke of Rothesay*. But owing to dense fog it didn't sail until the morning, the sea was as calm as a millpond but very misty all the way which meant we only went at half speed, and did not arrive till around 4pm. After a meal we boarded the train and travelled through the night getting to Hannover at 9am, where we were picked up and got to Dünsen in time for lunch. It has been arranged that we shall be handing over the work here to a COBSRA team in the next couple of days. We don't yet know where we are going, but have to report to 292 (P) Det. Mil. Gov. who will give us our instructions, so we have to wait and see.

No 2 Relief Section, Friends Ambulance Unit, BAOR [Hannover], 7 January 1946

Just a line to let you know the Section has left Dünsen and to give you my new address. We have to collect our own mail, but the Army Post Office is only 200 yards around the corner.

In accordance with the change in FAU policy the Section has been moved away from DP work to be involved with German civilian relief. We have settled into two houses about 2 kms. from the city centre – typical German style suburbia, and little damaged. Mil. Gov. has asked us to look into the Youth Organisation situation in the whole of the city. With the demise of the Hitler Youth the German local government, churches and other interested bodies are very keen to get something which meets Mil. Gov. regulations, into place as soon as possible.There has obviously been a great deal of talking going on, but our first task is to discover what is actually already in being. I think the local organisations may have been waiting to get the nod from Mil. Gov. before proceeding with their plans, if so with our arrival at Mil. Gov.'s request they now appear to have it. Tomorrow David Curtis and Martin Southwood are to meet with a Pastor Wolfe who the City has put in charge of Youth work... We are to have a new team leader, James Atkins, although David will remain deputy leader. James may have been chosen as he was formerly a teacher and will have some experience of working with children. I know him as he was the Section Leader when I was at Bangour Hospital in Scotland, but since then he has been doing relief work in France with Michael Cadbury. He is a very nice person, quietly spoken, and I am sure we shall get on well. So it's all change with a big challenge ahead. I will let you know how things progress... I am enclosing a letter for Daddy from Franz Link *[a German friend of my father's]*. It came through the German post to one of the German women who work for us, but not in its own envelope, and there was no sender's address, only Munich.

No 2 Relief Section, Friends Ambulance Unit, BAOR [Hannover], 10 January 1946

I have to say I'm quite glad to leave DP work, as I think there is greater need among the local German population. There is a great deal of damage in the city and many people are living under very difficult circumstances, often in cellars of bombed buildings, a public transport system which is struggling to recover, very many without work as businesses have not yet started up again, little confidence in the currency, far too low a food ration, not knowing what the future holds and so on. However, many seem resilient and prepared to work hard and to make the most of their opportunity to establish a democracy... To date we have mostly been going round the city talking to those who are involved in youth work, and have discovered that the churches are the most active, both Caritas Verband (Catholic) and the Lutheran Church have youth sections, and the Social Democrat Party are running a youth club for working class children, which they widely announced is non-political. There were, of course, a number of sports clubs of various kinds and they a trying to re-establish themselves. Interestingly, a group of older men are trying to set up a Boy Scout troop, but are not having much success as Mil. Gov. considers this too paramilitary! We also understand that the very recently formed Communist Party has a Young Communist League but have yet to make contact, they tend to keep a low profile. While political activity is now permitted there seems to be a lack of confidence at present to embark on it, but I can't see that lasting very long. Clearly there are many difficulties to overcome, finding accommodation, equipment, supplies, and to get Mil. Gov. ratification to start up. We had a bit of luck in tracing some 'frozen' Hitler Youth equipment which has been made available to us.

Mil. Gov. is being very helpful but they emphasise that we must keep a watchful eye out to make sure that there is no undercover Nazi influences in these new organisations. It is most encouraging that we have been so warmly welcomed by church leaders and that there are so many volunteers coming forward and wanting to help at all levels. We have been not a little surprised to find how enthusiastic most people are at our being here and appear not to be at all offended at what could be considered interference in their affairs.

In addition Mil. Gov. has now asked us to review the situation with regard to children's hospitals, cripples' homes, places for child delinquents and similar institutions. We have many places still to report on, but everywhere the main lack is supplies of all kinds, and the little help available to repair bombed buildings, still many boarded windows and roofs requiring retiling. The acute shortage of transport is a major problem. So the outlook for our immediate future is 'very busy'.

No 2 Relief Section, Friends Ambulance Unit [Hannover], 19 January 1946

I have received your letter to Franz Link and will send it to him by the same process. As you know service personnel may not use the civilian postal service which is struggling to cope. The German women who work for us are registered for their mail at the local post-amt *[post office]*. I got one of them to write her name and address on the back of your envelope, before posting it to him. He put his reply in an envelope addressed to her and she then gave it to me to send on to you. The only difficulty would be if we had to move. As I write the snow is falling quite thickly and I am glad to be in a reasonably warm house... Thank you for sounding out Lewis's *[H.K. Lewis, medical publishers and booksellers; after my release in the autumn of 1947 I took up a position with them]* and talking further with Eric Barnard *[a cousin, who was a director of Edward Barnard & Sons, silversmiths in London]*. I do really appreciate your help in considering my future and I'm sorry I'm so indecisive at the moment, but I expect it will all come clearer soon. As to my immediate future, a decision is to be made this month about a successor body to the Unit. A senior Gordon Square staff member has been making the rounds of many sections enquiring how many would actually join it if it was established and so on. I have not decided what to do yet, although in my mind I would like to work out my time here continuing what I'm doing at present, as yet, of course, there is no idea what the new body would do, or where it will operate...

We and others have been visiting every charitable and local government organisation in the city to discover the schemes they are operating – hospitals, homes, schools, etc. It would seem there is no shortage of enthusiastic people with ideas and plans, but the obstacles to putting them into place is immense – particularly supplies and premises in good repair. We were shown a room, little larger than an average sitting room, only half filled with boxes of supplies of all sorts. This was the entire supplies of the German Red Cross for Hannover and its environs! When one knows the need, it is tragic – the conditions in the transit camps for refugees from the Russian Zone, the hundreds trying to live in the air raid shelter under the main railway station, schools without heating, or books or even paper and pencils, hospitals and homes without enough fuel to run the laundries, I could go on and on. Paramount is supplies of all kinds. We have been allocated about three tons of supplies for all of Hannover, but how do you find the greatest need? Do hospitals get first call on soap, is it worth giving one pencil to a school of 200 children? We are in discussion with a Dr Nagel, the Chief Public Health Officer for the city of Hannover, to try to work all this out and form a comprehensive plan. It may seem a rather cumbersome way of going about things but

Outside the Hannover billet, Ganghoferstrasse: Gordon Taylor, David Davies, Clifford, James Atkins. The team worked with local authorities and charities to establish a non-political, non-sectarian youth club; carried out a survey of the District's hospitals for the British Control Commission; and helped set up a holiday feeding scheme for malnourished city children on the Frisian island of Langeoog.

it at least assures that nothing gets onto the black market, which is very widespread.

Others in the Section are still involved with the youth work. It would appear that most of the clubs that have got off the ground are run by the churches, both Protestant and Catholic, and among many other things have asked us for bibles. It occurred to me whether Auntie Madeline, who works I believe for the Baptist Missionary Society would be interested to know this? The bibles should be in German which may be a difficulty. The sports clubs seem well attended but again the little equipment they have is very run down and inadequate. The men who wanted to start a boy scout movement, which they would call Deutsche Jugendschaft, are still persevering with the authorities, which you may recall have banned the idea as being too paramilitary. The Social Democrat Party, which has come very much to the fore since the war ended, are running a very well attended youth organisation for working class children which they claim abides by Mil. Gov. regulations and has no political bias. They say they give talks based on the 'four freedoms' designed to remove all traces of Nazi thinking. Another individual who has come to our attention is trying to re-establish the Youth Hostels Association; he used to work for the Jurgendherbergenverband *[German Youth Hostels Association]* before the war. The main difficulty is the lack of premises, those hostels that survived the war were mostly requisitioned for other purposes and their release would have to be negotiated. I expect Jack Catchpool *[a Welwyn Quaker and involved with the YHA in Britain]*, who I hear has been in France on a similar mission, may like to know of this interest in Germany.

No 2 Relief Section, FAU, BAOR [Hannover], 29 January 1946

Sorry to hear you have had 'flu. Fortunately we all keep very well, maybe because it's so cold and we are out of doors most of the time. A large canal runs only a few yards from our house and at weekends it is black with skaters. It's a big thing over here, and I have to say the girls look very attractive with little woollen caps, beautifully patterned jerseys, woollen gloves, and short skirts. I wish I could skate! The weather is pretty cold, but our fuel ration seems to be enough to keep the house reasonably warm, although lukewarm not hot baths have to be on a strict rota. Food is ample, cereals for breakfast, but only with tinned milk. Fresh vegetables, but rather too many onions and carrots, meat almost every day, and Australian butter, and Army baked bread... I see the Conscientious Objectors bill is coming up for debate in the Lords next week, that will be interesting... I saw something rather unusual the other day which may interest John *[Freda's husband was a train buff]*. A long goods train was

passing over a railway bridge near here with all the usual German rolling stock, occasionally a truck marked 'USA Transport Corps', but suddenly an LMS coal truck went by with a notice 'Not to be used between
Finchley and Hampstead'. A bit off its usual beat I would have thought!

We have mostly completed all the visiting and interviewing of charitable institutions and made our reports to Mil. Gov. It is very frustrating
but there doesn't seem to be a great deal more we can do. They are all
operating as well as they can with the staff they need, it is just this over-
riding need for supplies of all sorts. It is no longer a case of us doing the
bandaging but us giving them the bandages so they can do it themselves,
if you follow. Occasionally we can help out with transport, but mostly
it is a case of keeping up the visiting to encourage and show someone
is interested, make lists of needs and see if Mil. Gov. can do anything
about it. We also find we can have a sort of liaison role between the
organisations and the British authorities, and have helped with getting
requisitioned buildings released and a licence for a Pastor's car. We also
distribute as fairly as we can the few supplies we do get.

I was alone in our small office the other day when a lady came in,
who turned out to be a German Quaker, Dr Frau von Loebell. She spoke
good English and was a close friend of Corder Catchpool. We had a most
interesting conversation as she had lived in England for a time and visited Welwyn Garden City and knew Dr Ralph Crowley. She had paid us
a visit, because she thought we might be connected with Friends, and
had plans to start a small co-ed school on the lines of English Friends'
schools and also a nightly youth club. Very ambitious and expensive
ideas to have at the present time. There was little practical help I could
offer, although I was able to give her a few addresses both here and in
England. We also had a visit from the son of Pastor Wilhelm Mensching
*[a religious pacifist who was a leader of the German branch of the Fellowship
of Reconciliation and visited Woodbrooke in 1928; he later became a Quaker, I
believe]*. He is the medical director of the large Norstadt Krankenhaus in
the city. Like his father he remained a pacifist throughout the war, con-
sistently refused to ever give a Nazi salute and although of military age
managed to remain untouched. With his father he was well respected
and much loved as a village doctor, and as I understand it a local police
officer never delivered his call up papers but kept them locked up in
his desk in the police station! *[I wish I could verify this story]*. He was so
very pleased to meet up with us and invited David to a meeting he was
arranging of German Friends, pacifists and other like minded people,
and hoped he could give a talk about our work in Hannover…

No 2 Relief Section, Friends Ambulance Unit, BAOR [Hannover], 6 February 1946

Weather quite mild, although we had a terrible storm three days ago and a fierce wind brought down walls from some of the more unstable ruins, blocking some of the minor streets, so all the clearing up has started again. At least it got rid of the last vestiges of snow. Little work at the moment, so David has gone on leave and Arthur goes next week. Martin, very impressively, has given three talks in German, to youth organisations, mainly on English youth clubs. I'm enclosing three photos taken some months ago by George Champion, they are my only copies so please hang on to them... Been listening to some of the UNA broadcasts – Bevin is being very frank and outspoken to the Russians, isn't he?

The Reinwald family with Clifford and ambulance, and message of thanks on the back of the photo. Their father, an anti-Nazi Lutheran pastor, had been liberated from a concentration camp in the Russian Zone. His wife managed to get the three children to the British Zone and then returned to fetch her husband who was too sick to travel alone. While she was away the FAU team 'looked out' for the children, giving them food parcels etc.

No 2 Relief Section, Friends Ambulance Unit, BAOR [Hannover], 10 February 1946

Very stormy and wet the last few days, but strangely it snows at night, which leaves so much slush that the planes can't land or take off at the airfield, and two of the temporary bridges on roads leading out of the city have collapsed. The Royal Engineers with German labourers have been busy trying to repair them. The mail is taking a long time at the moment, which is understandable... We are keeping fit but 'flu is widespread in the German population and the authorities, with memories of the epidemic of 1918 in mind, have forbidden all British troops to go to local concerts, cinemas, etc... At long last we have received a few supplies, Ovaltine, Horlicks, cod liver oil and soap which we are hastening to get out to children's hospitals and the like... I received a nice letter from Brian Barnett to say he had had the privilege of reading some of my letters home and was enthusiastic about what I was doing... I will reply as soon as I can, but if you see him let him know that I appreciated him writing... Yes, I have seen Deryck Moore recently, he is based at British Red Cross HQ at Vlotho, but spends quite a bit of time travelling around visiting the various Sections. I haven't seen Giles Cooper since the Antwerp days, now nearly a year ago, but I had a joint letter from Jocelyn and Alison *[his sisters, both at St Christopher School]*. No news of Reg or Gaydu. The FAU conference didn't come to a conclusion about a follow up organisation, but set up a committee to examine the idea further. It would appear that the British Red Cross might have to withdraw some of their teams as recruitment is falling off and others have already left for home, but have said they would welcome any FAU members who wish to stay on when their Sections close.

No 2 Relief Section, Friends Ambulance Unit, BAOR [Hannover], 19 February 1946

Well I'm supposed to be adult now *[It was my 21st birthday on the 18th of February]* but it doesn't feel any different! Thanks for the telegram and the parcel with the cake, altogether I had 14 letters and cards. I'll need some addresses so I can thank people. Arthur *[Jewson]* laid on a special meal in the evening, with a cake made by the German women, a sort of sponge actually with vanilla and chocolate cream in 'whirligigs' spread over the top, and even a small vase of 'pussy willow' on the table. He had also managed to get a bottle of champagne and a moselle wine. The whole team gave me a very nice wooden chess set, so I had to reply with a little speech of thanks, and then they all drank to my good health, after which most of us piled into a truck and went off to the cinema to see *Music for the Millions*. When we got back we had coffee and biscuits before going to bed. You couldn't ask for more, could you?

No 2 Relief Section, Friends Ambulance Unit, BAOR [Hannover], 23 February 1946

We had a visit from Michael Rowntree, last week, who if you remember took over from Gerald Gardiner. He came to inform us of the present situation regarding the closure of the Unit. It has been decided that two Sections are to return to England in the next two weeks, but the future of our Section depends on whether Friends Relief Service will wish to take over any of the work we have been doing here and have the resources to do so. FRS is not taking over whole teams only individual members on recommendation. I could transfer if I wish, then if they do take up the work here, in all probability I could stay in the same job, but I don't really know and we will have to wait and see. This will all be decided before June, but if it doesn't happen I could be home before then. In case this happens I am sending a few parcels back with books and so on. I am also returning the balance of my money, £7, I am unlikely to need such a large sum out here, maybe you could put it in my Post Office savings. This has to go through HQ at Vlotho, then Gordon Square, so it may take some time... Now about this information your friend in South America is seeking, particularly about the present feelings of the German public. What I am aware of is a bit secondhand, as my German is not adequate enough for deep conversation at this level, but I'll do what I can. As you know I wrote a long letter to Brian Barnett recently, mainly giving my impressions of the conditions here and our work, so maybe some of that will suffice.

No 2 Relief Section, Friends Ambulance Unit, BAOR [Hannover], 27 February 1946

Weather has been very changeable, heavy rain and high winds, followed by snow, then almost springlike, before more snow. We took advantage of the milder spell to change into our new kit and play a game of football, subsequently we are all a bit stiff!... John Freshwater is going home today. Although only 21 he is leaving the Unit to take up some paid hospital work, while studying at night school. He was one of the original team. I have taken on his work of tracing missing persons on behalf of the Red Cross and other 'contact' jobs that come along. For example, this week I delivered some letters from a group of Norwegians to a German they

Studio portrait of Clifford: Hannover, March 1946

had known before the war. Myrtle Wright, a Quaker relief worker in Norway, brought the letters with her and took them to FAU HQ at Gordon Square, from where they were sent on to us. *[Myrtle Wright later wrote of her experiences in a book,* Norwegian Diary 1940–1945, *published in 1974. She was involved in the non-violent resistance movement with Diderich and Sigrid Lund, helping people, many Jewish, to escape to neutral Sweden. Eventually they had to escape themselves over the same route.]* The recipient *[I never recorded his name]* turned out to be a communist and an ex-concentration camp victim. I had a conversation with him as far as my limited German went, he particularly wanted to know about the FAU, and was most impressed that allowance was made for conscientious objectors in England…

As John was going home and David and I both had 21st birthdays, it was decided to hold a party. John Tanner has a girl friend who is studying at a gymnastic training school in Hannover, and she brought a number of her friends along. We had quite a party, and I found a very nice girl to take home. We got on so well that we are going to meet again next weekend, she is still in her first year at the training school and only speaks about as much English as I speak German. I think life is getting more interesting out here at the moment!

No 2 Relief Section, Friends Ambulance Unit, BAOR [Hannover], 6 March 1946

I'm sorry but I can't be more helpful about Frau Dr von Loebel. She only contacted us to see if we could help with the school she is running at Gehrden, some 18 kms south of Hannover. Apart from giving her some addresses in England we were not able to provide the kind of assistance she was seeking, mainly financial. So we won't really have any reason to meet her again, although I could always pay her a visit if you would like me to. As far as I can recall from my conversation with her, she said she knew Corder Catchpool from the 'Berlin days' before the war, and Ralph Crowley in 1936 when she visited WGC and talked about their newly built house at Tewin. I could always forward a letter if you wish. By the way I understand the civilian post between Germany and Britain is supposed to be starting up from April 1st... I had to drive south today to Hameln, the snow was really thick there and the surrounding hills looked so beautiful. I passed through several fascinating villages with no apparent damage... We have been issuing cartons of nourishing drinks to various homes and institutions in our area, and we have had some delightful letters of thanks. I must quote from one which is priceless – 'Many thanks for your kind peasant of nowisching food which we got from you for our home of old people and children. Our ill and old people were very much enjoyed of the surprise we cond make them by your lovely supply. Our children were especially enjoyed of the beautiful cocoa which out little got for the first time in their life. For all good things once more our best thanks'. We have many other letters one or two from the children themselves... By the way my girl friend's name is Renate and we have met several times now.

No 2 Relief Section, Friends Ambulance Unit, BAOR [Hannover], 11 March 1946

Work continuing much the same. This latest cut in the German food ration to 1,050 calories is very serious. When the people in Belsen were actually being fed they were getting about 800 calories, and that was virtually a starvation diet. The average British 'Tommy' is friendly towards the Germans, and although it is strictly illegal are giving some of their NAAFI items to people they know. I have heard that the British Army ration may be reduced, whether this is to stop surplus being given away or just because they have to, I don't know. I can't help feeling that as long as they have food and the Germans don't they will continue to give it away. John was in Celle last week, which is a small town of some

20,000, and was talking to the Town Major who told him that he had been inundated by applications from British soldiers wanting to marry German girls...

No 2 Relief Section, Friends Ambulance Unit, [Hannover], 18 March 1946

We have had some sunshine in the last two days and I didn't even need a coat on. What a difference it makes, all the passers-by in the city seemed to be smiling. I went to a German production of *Madam Butterfly* at the Herrenhausen Theatre. I saw *Carmen* there some weeks ago, they were very good... Part of the British Red Cross work is to keep in touch with British subjects for the Foreign Office, so I have been doing a bit of this recently. If their whereabouts are not already known it means tracing them from their last address before the war. Then visit them to see how they are coping, sort out any problems and provide them with a food parcel. I don't feel too happy about this as I don't see why we should discriminate in their favour just because they were born in England, but chose to stay in Germany. One old lady I visited was 87 and had lived in Germany for 50 years. Very contemptuous of what she called the 'North-cliffe' papers and said her father had been the Governor of Canada!... The German food situation is bleak. General Templar of the British Control Commission who addressed a meeting of Section leaders in Vlotho, said that unless more wheat could be brought in the calorific value of the ration would have to drop again, starting next month. It is only 1,050 at the moment and it is only at this level because potatoes can still be made available. He went on to say that there is just enough wheat in the world to meet the present demand, but if one country has more than their share, then people will starve, and the first will be Germany. Britain depends almost entirely on supplies from America, Canada and Australia, but he believes USA and Argentina, still have spare capacity...Renate invited me around to see her family and I stayed for a meal, but I took a loaf of bread and some tins with me. When I saw what they were actually eating I was ashamed. They only get one slice of black bread a meal and one and a half potatoes a day. Milk only twice a week. Vegetables are not rationed but can only be obtained after queuing endlessly, unless you can grow your own. Coffee is very scarce and then only ersatz. The family, her mother and two older sisters, were all very nice. Her father died in 1938, he was a schoolmaster. The older sister, Annelotte, is married, but her husband is still missing in Russia, they hope he is a PoW, but have had no news. Gisela, the other sister, is engaged to Elmar, who was in the German Navy, but is now in the furniture business. I met him too...

No 2 Relief Section, Friends Ambulance Unit, [Hannover], 30 March 1946

Glorious weather. Several games of football, and last Sunday John *[Tanner]*, Gordon *[Taylor]* and I packed up some sandwiches, picked the girls up and went off for the day. By the river Aller where some pine woods sweep down to the river bank *[see photos pp.124–5]*. If it had been a little warmer we could have gone swimming. We didn't see anybody there all day. Came back to our house and all had supper together, a lovely break... We hear that a successor body to the FAU will definitely go ahead now, but no actual details as yet. Roger Stanger has got a job with the British Red Cross out here and will get £3.10s a week. This is really worth thinking about as I could do the same and the money sounds attractive... I enclose some comments I have written out for your friend, Herzfeld. I hope it will do, but there's not much about the feelings of the German people... The civilian post to Germany starts on April 1st, postage for a letter will be 5d or 80pfg.

No 2 Relief Section, Friends Ambulance Unit, [Hannover], 31 March 1946

Although I only wrote yesterday I forgot to include the Youth Hostels information and then Mummy's letter came this morning. The address of the organiser in Hannover is Erich Schlicker, Hannover-Herrenhausen, Hegeblachstr, 32. I had a letter from him saying that he now had three groups up and running and inviting us to pay a visit. He is only the Geschäftsführer for Hannover Province, and said he didn't know what is happening elsewhere in Germany. The printed heading on the letter reads – Landesverband Hannover in Hauptverband für Jugendherbergen und Jugendwandern, with the same triangle motif as in England...

I'll have a go at trying to find this girl for Elsie Smith. This tracing work is taking up a lot of my time now, mainly official cases forwarded to us from the Red Cross. It requires searching the records of the German Police and the old Air Raid authority records, unfortunately towards the end of the war when things got very chaotic the records become more haphazard and less reliable. However, I am pleased to say I managed to conclude five cases out of seven last week, one I had been tracing for 3 or 4 weeks. It was particularly difficult as the usual sources didn't throw up any leads, but eventually I found someone living in a cellar in a nearby street, who had known the family and had the mother's address in the American Zone. I wrote to her and she replied with her daughter's address, and although it was some 30 kms away I managed to pay a visit.

Some cases are very sad. From a Jewish family of four only a little girl of eleven remained who I found was still living with friends who had taken her in, presumably when the rest of the family were taken away. At least she now has her Aunt's address in England. In these cases I only have to write out a report of what I have or haven't found and send it back to the Red Cross.

Many years later, I discovered that the sheltering of Jewish people, particularly children, by friends and neighbours had occurred more often than was generally realised. For some time after the war there was still a reluctance to talk about what they had done. In his book The Righteous, *Martin Gilbert estimates that though one hundred and seventy thousand of Berlin's pre-war Jewish population either emigrated or were killed, about 2,000 survived in hiding in the city. They could not have done this without help. He said that one of them had written, 'We will never know how many Berliners had the decency and courage to save their Jewish co-citizens from the Nazis – twenty thousand, thirty thousand? We don't need to know the number in order to pay homage to this untypical, admirable minority'. Leslie Wilson in an Afterword to his moving novel,* Saving Rafael *(Andersen Press, 2009) wrote: 'it is known that many German Quakers did help and hide Jews. One of them, Elizabeth Abegg, turned her little apartment into a temporary shelter and assembly point for Jews who had gone underground, sharing her rations and obtaining forged papers for them. She has been honoured by the Jewish Holocaust memorial organisation Yad Vashem, and the city of Berlin has put a plaque on the house where she lived. One of the people she helped called her "A light in the darkness of Nazi Germany"'. According to Leonard Gross's book,* The Last Jews in Berlin, *many were smuggled out of Germany by the Swedish Lutheran Church.*

No 2 Relief Section, Friends Ambulance Unit, BAOR [Hannover], 10 April 1946

I enclose a letter for Elsie Smith about the girl she wants to contact. Sorry for the delay but it had its difficulties. I couldn't find the address, as the whole area was rubble, but I got near enough to satisfy myself that the house no longer existed. The register of bomb victims at the air raid records also drew a blank, so I went back to the locality and started enquiring in the shops that still remained there. Reasoning that if she was still alive and in the area she would have to be registered to get her food rations somewhere. Strangely enough it was not at a food shop but a watch repairer that I got a lead. They had a clock in for repair under the right name, Boetcher, but no address. The shop person promised to get an address when the clock was collected. When I went back they provided an address which I visited but it turned out to be her sister, who told me that the girl, a woman now, Elsie was enquiring about was dead. As it was obviously a very emotional situation I didn't enquire any further, so I don't know the circumstances, but she spoke good English and said she had lived in England for some time, and agreed to write the letter to Elsie, which I enclose...

Further to Jack Catchpool and Herr Schlicker, he might like to know that he arranged for Martin *[Southwood]* and myself to visit one or two buildings that had been Youth Hostels before the war. One was derelict, which in a way is hopeful, another is being used as a home for TB patients, and another is part of a refugee camp. Herr Schlicker seemed quite hopeful that they would all be released in time, but they are hopelessly without any equipment or furniture. I enclose photos of three we visited at Hameln, Springe and Mellendorf, and he is arranging for another visit next week, which will include Steinhude. It is difficult to see how we can help, although since our visit Martin has managed to get some ex-Hitler Youth wooden double bunks released...

With the weather being so nice John, David, Gordon and myself again went picnicking by the river Aller with the girls, again it was not warm enough to swim, but we had a lovely walk... On Monday I had to drive down to Bielefeld, some 80 miles, a nice stretch of autobahn through pleasant countryside, but the town itself is damaged... The successor body to the FAU has now been established and is to be called the FAU Post War Service. *[The FAU Post War and International Service came*

The Youth Hostels Association in Britain asked for a survey of former Deutsche Jugendherberger premises and how they had been used. Left: Mellendorf. Above: Hameln.

into being in June 1946, when the FAU formally closed. The story of its work can be found in a book FAU: the Third Generation *by Roger Bush.]* Two more FAU Sections have now been closed, those members not returning to England are joining the new body or Friends Relief Service or BRC. I have to make up my mind soon. David will be leaving the Section soon to become the Liaison Officer for all COBSRA teams in Hannover Province working on German Welfare. The post was previously held by Donald Ratcliffe who is going home, he was 28 but David is only 21.

No 2 Relief Section, Friends Ambulance Unit, BAOR [Hannover], 17 April 1946

Yesterday, we had a visit from Mike Rowntree (FAU) and Eric Cleaver (FRS) to discuss the future. It was decided that our work didn't warrant a whole new FRS section compared to the needs of places like Aachen and in the Ruhr. FRS has very limited personnel and cannot take over the work of more than two FAU sections. However, it was recognised that our commitments here would have to be wound down slowly, and probably handed over to interested persons in Mil. Gov. It will become a temporary FRS section until the autumn when its work will be reviewed, apart from James and Martin, who will be seconded to FRS, the rest of us will either go home or join the new FAU post-war service, or BRC. I now have to get fixed up with one of these organisations before June.

David, as I think I told you, is now the Red Cross Liaison Officer for

Clifford relaxing in the garden at Ganghoferstrasse, April 1946

Hannover Province, so James *[Atkins]* has become Section Leader. David asked me to take over his work with British subjects living here. This is really consular work, but I, in turn, have to hand it over to Mil. Gov. before I leave. I visited a Capt. Marsh, who will be taking this on, and become an acting temporary vice-consul in the process! As far as I could see he had very little to do anyway, and didn't seem too interested in adding to it, all the time I was with him he would only talk about duck and game shooting. Not quite my area of expertise!... As a final fling David, Gordon and I are taking 72 hours leave over Easter at the Bad Harzburg officers leave hotel, should be an experience.

No 2 Relief Section, Friends Ambulance Unit, BAOR [Hannover], 25 April 1946

I enclose a letter and photo from your friend Franz Link, which arrived yesterday through our system. Perhaps he doesn't know the civilian mail is working now?... We had an enjoyable time on leave. The hotel was rather posh, terrific meals with wine, even our shoes got cleaned over night. There were billiard and table tennis tables, and we enjoyed some superb walks in the Harz mountains, very wooded with delightful streams. We came down one mountain by cable car, and noticed that the ski slopes are now being got ready. The mountain air was good, but the evenings were spent rather differently, dancing and drinking. On the last night we visited the Barbarina Night Club in the Harzburger Hof hotel, it was British run, but the bands and cabarets were mostly local people. I'm glad to have had the experience, but I'm not sure it is really my thing... Reg came over from Frankfurt the other day. He has left the FAU now and works as a driver for an IGCR official and goes all over the place – Berlin, Prague, Vienna and Switzerland. I had a phone call the other evening from Peter Lowenfeld, who you may remember was one of the German Jewish refugee children at Chris, I think his mother was a doctor specialising in child matters. He is a now known as Lt. Lowell, but is actually working for the Control Commission as a liaison officer on economic matters at Bad Pyrmont, I suppose his fluent German is useful.

No 2 Relief Section, Friends Ambulance Unit, BAOR [Hannover], 2 May 1946

I've been thinking more seriously about transferring to the BRC and decided to go and talk with their Personnel Officer at the BRC HQ in Vlotho, in the same building as the FAU HQ. He was quite friendly and after talking over my work and experience offered me a job as a Welfare Officer at £4.10 a week. There were no vacancies in tracing bureau work.

The appointment has to be ratified in London, but I think this is just a formality. Roger has joined as a Transport Officer at the same rate of pay. I will probably be posted to a team in the Ruhr, but will stay in Hannover till early June, when the section becomes an FRS team. On the whole I think this is the best solution. I am very interested in the current situation in Germany and would like to stay out here while I work out the rest of my time. I feel the experience I have already gained of German welfare work can still be of some use. Secondly I don't want to leave just yet, as you may have guessed I am becoming very attached to Renate, she is such a nice girl and I wish you could meet her. I think you would notice a change in me... Although very different to the FAU I think I shall get on alright in the BRC, but it remains to be seen where I shall be posted.

Clifford and Renate outside the FAU billet in Ganghoferstrasse,
Hannover, April 1946

The Section gets ever smaller. Gordon, Donald *[Ratcliffe]* and Geoff *[Wareing]* left last week. David still lives with us but works all day in the Mil. Gov. offices in Hannover. Roger leaves to join a BRC team this week and Arthur goes home in a fortnight. That leaves only six, of which only Martin and myself are originals. FRS take over the Section in June when James and Martin remain, John is getting an earlier release as a medical student, and when I go that will be the end of FAU Section 2... You may have read in the newspapers of a large fire in Stirling House, where David works, fortunately he was in the other end of the building but had to be evacuated, apparently, two German clerks died... The food situation remains very critical, but amazingly they still seem to be able to laugh about it. Renate told me this joke is going the rounds. The present ration group is 89, if there is anybody left alive by group 90 they will be prosecuted for having dealt on the black market...

No2 Relief Section, Friends Ambulance Unit [Hannover], 17 May 1946

Team now reduced to six, but still trying to keep the work load up, another unit is now collecting our rations for us, and we are considering hiring local German labour to service our vehicles. Surprisingly we are now getting supplies through more frequently, which means extra work to distribute them equitably... My personal plans have not progressed as I have heard nothing further from the Red Cross, similarly Roger who applied long before me is still with us. The Section becomes an FRS one on 5 June, but I don't suppose they will mind me hanging on here until I get my Red Cross posting. I would still like to have some home leave before I transfer. The weather has been really warm recently and being by the river at the weekend has meant we have got quite brown. Now that Gordon has left John has joined me in my room, and every morning we go for a run followed by a cold bath... At the moment we have an interesting Swede staying with us, he is surveying child feeding in Hannover and has just come straight from the European Food talks in Atlantic City. He worked for the Swedish Red Cross throughout the war and saw the situation from both sides. The incidence of TB is now widespread in Germany and Mil. Gov. is very concerned. We have been procuring statistics on the disease from hospitals, factories, schools and so on, apart from the food situation it is the most dangerous threat to the German people, not helped, of course, by the short rations and crowded living conditions. With Mil. Gov., local authorities and Swedish Red Cross we are drawing up plans to take groups of children from schools in Hannover to the Frisian Islands for five weeks at a time, hoping that

2 FAU arranged an evening party at their billet, and invited several students from the Reichman School for women gymnastic teachers. Other social occasions followed, including picnics by the river Aller near Celle. Left to right: Gordon Taylor, Marianne, John Tanner, Clifford; boy unidentified.

better food and fresh air will help build up resistance to the disease. The Frisian Islands are undamaged and have many empty hotels and guest houses. David and a Colonel Beamish from Mil. Gov. made a recce last week and the arrangements are now complete. On Monday I shall be the only Britisher on a train, which will leave from Hannover Central station, with the first batch of 900 hundred children and several dozen volunteer German staff. Apart from being available in case liaison with British forces is needed, it is intended I should stay on the island, Langeoog, for 3 or 4 days. I will have to write a report for British Red Cross HQ, on how it all went. John will drive up and fetch me back later. I can't see I shall have much to do except observe, so it could be quite a rest with fresh ozone air.

No 2 Relief Section, Friends Ambulance Unit, BAOR [Hannover], 26 May 1946

I expect you would like to know how it all went. The Frisian Islands are off the north German coast, although those to the west are Dutch territory. From the Weser estuary going west, Langeoog, the largest, lies between Borkum and Spiekeroog. The special train left Hannover at 8 pm and I shared a compartment with three of the German organisers, Herr Mund

Left to right: Clifford, Renate, John Tanner, Marianne, David Curtis, Uschi, Gordon Taylor. John continued his medical studies in England and married Marianne in 1947. David emigrated to New Zealand and became headmaster of a boys' school. Gordon studied to qualify as a State Registered Nurse.

(Hannover Gesundsheitsamt), Pastor Schwedhelm (Innere Mission) and an official from the Deutsches Rotes Kreuz. The conditions on the train were not good, as the windows in the carriages had little glass, simply filled with cardboard and wood, which meant the ventilation could not be controlled. As there were no light bulbs it was very dark and the atmosphere became stuffy and unpleasant. While these conditions are not unusual for trains at the moment, it wasn't very desirable for the undernourished children, and the nurses and helpers had a difficult time. We did not arrive until 8.30 am the next morning, and it took most of the day to ship the children across to the island on air-sea rescue launches, as only a few could be carried at a time. Langeoog had a peacetime population of around 700, but many were evacuated during the war, compared with most of Germany it seems a paradise.

Its only occupation was as a holiday resort and so every other building seems to be a hotel or guest house, and there are also a number of empty, undamaged houses. Although we have brought nearly a 1,000 children there still seems room for more. The island seems mostly grass covered sand dunes and lovely beaches, but I wasn't able to see very much as it rained most of the time or was shrouded in a wet mist. John drove up the following day with more German officials, Baroness von

Knigge (German Red Cross) and a Dr Meyer and Dr Depuhl, from local government. John and I stayed with them all in a hotel which had been set aside for us. We insisted on sharing our rations with them, which was very much appreciated, and was supplemented with local fish and omelettes made from seagull's eggs! Milk and cheese is plentiful as there are cows on the island. With the help of Swedish Red Cross supplies it is planned to provide the children with 2,000 calories a day. We were shown round the buildings where the children are being housed and were impressed how everything had been arranged under such difficult circumstances. At supper on our last evening, Dr Depuhl made a speech thanking us for all the help we had provided and presented us with the Langeoog enamelled badge *[which I still have]*.

On returning to Hannover we wrote a report on the scheme for Mil. Gov. It was well received and they said consideration would be given to our comments on the travelling arrangements. We had suggested that a bus service on two successive days might be better than the night train. If it was scheduled to fit in with tides, it might be possible to avoid the children having to hang about so long on the cold and wet quay side and make it less hectic to get the children all settled in at once on arrival. I am due to see Colonel Beamish tomorrow to discuss this... No further news as to when I might be joining the Red Cross. David, who is also joining, spoke with a Mr Aspinell, the Personnel Officer, who was hopeful we would be in by 1st June. That remains to be seen. I understand eleven ex-FAU have been accepted for transfer...

I was round at Renate's last night, Gisela's fiancé Elmar was there. He seems a nice fellow, but is happy to be out of the German Navy now. I think he was on a minesweeper, mainly off the coasts of France and Norway, but also visited the Channel Islands. He is strongly opposed to the division of Germany into zones, and particularly the loss of East Prussia and other eastern territories to Poland, as these areas are Germany's main source of agricultural produce... By the way, please stop sending the monthly payments through the bank, as the Unit Financial Dept. closes down on June 30th.

No 2 Relief Section, Friends Relief Service, BAOR [Hannover], 2 June 1946

Well as you will see from the address this is now an FRS Section. The only difference is that one FRS member has joined from England, and James, John, Martin and Morgan *[Johnson]* have sewn on Friends Relief Service shoulder flashes. Arthur and David Davies have received their demob notices and will be leaving for home next week. That leaves

Roger, David Curtis and myself who are now paid members of the British Red Cross. Roger has been posted to a team in the Ruhr and David is remaining here as he is the Liaison Officer in Hannover. BRC HQ at Vlotho think it will be alright for me to take my home leave before being posted, but they are waiting until Mr Aspinell returns. So leave the door open I could be home anytime... Work continues... my talk with Colonel Beamish was good, but he didn't think the buses idea was a possibility as there is a crucial shortage and enough could not be released from their daily use as commuter transport. However, he decided to travel up and have a look himself, as he says it is planned to have several more groups going there before the summer is over. A Mr Petit, head of Public Health Welfare for the Control Commission congratulated me on a very lucid report. However, I have now handed these responsibilities over to John who is staying on in the FRS team until his class B release comes through, as a medical student he can go earlier. A Miss McFarland of the British Interests Branch at the Control Commission HQ, from whom I have been receiving instructions concerning British Subjects, came to see me. She said I had been a great help and was sorry to see me go... Martin's 'Quäkererholungsheim', in the Harz, for undernourished children from Hannover has received warm praise from Mil. Gov., and the TB survey is now finished and sent in to Mil. Gov. who have asked us to undertake a nutritional survey next. The 'searcher service' is ongoing, Jewish cases predominate now but mostly end sadly. The German police at the Central Police Records are quite helpful and have got to know me now, but I read that the Police Chief in Hannover has been sacked as a past Nazi.

The Jugenderholungsheim for undernourished children from Hannover, at Bocksweise in the Oberharz, established by 2 FAU with the DRK (Deutsche Rote Kreuz) in Spring 1946.

No 2 Relief Section, Friends Relief Service, BAOR
[Hannover], 9 June 1946

Well I'm still here, it was decided I shouldn't go on leave until I hear officially from the BRC. The Section is down to five, but still trying to meet commitments... Dreadful weather, very hot and sticky with regular thunderstorms, continental climate, I suppose... Last Friday I took a group of German Friends and others to a Whitsun conference at the Quäkerhaus in Bad Pyrmont. It was my first visit there and I found it all so familiar, just like before a session of our Yearly Meeting, everybody shaking hands and chattering away in groups. I was whisked away by Mary Friedrich, an English lady married to a German Quaker, Leonhard, who had recently been released from a concentration camp *[see Brenda Bailey, A Quaker Couple in Nazi Germany]*. They had sent their daughter, Brenda, to England just before the war started. She insisted on giving me a cup of tea in a typical Meeting House room with small tables covered in blue and white squared table cloths. She did remind me of Alice Catford *[a Welwyn Friend]*. As I had arranged to meet Peter Lowenfeld *[ex-Chris school friend]* on the way home I had to leave quite soon, but the Hannover Friends are staying for the week. Peter who is a captain now seemed pleased to see me and invited me to stay for supper. I had a three hour drive to do and it was well after mid-night before I got back... I've also had a letter from Gaydu, he is still in Italy, and is also a Captain.

Soon after writing the above letter I must have gone on home leave.

Clifford with his cousin Gwen Wills in Canadian Air Force uniform:
Welwyn Garden City, June 1946

No 2 Relief Section, Friends Relief Service, BAOR [Hannover], 3 July 1946

Just a short note to let you know I'm back in Hannover. I got in around midnight, tiring but not too bad. The crossing was smooth, but stepped into a sweltering continental summer, dripping with heat. It was frightful in the train but fortunately only four others in my carriage, one an overweight Major who looked as though he was melting, and talked about it being nothing to what he had experienced in India. Nothing from the BRC, although David thinks I might be asked to cover for him as the Liaison Officer as he is going on leave, but nothing definite. Renate is well, she seems to thrive on this hot weather.

After this I left the section and joined a British Red Cross team.

8. British Red Cross, Hildesheim

July to September 1946

146 Relief Section, British Red Cross, c/o 117 RB Det. Mil. Gov., BAOR, 6 July 1946

Well here I am with my new BRC Section in Hildesheim, which is about 26 kms. south of Hannover. It is a new Section which has only been out here five months, and has been in some sort of trouble resulting in the Section Leader resigning and three other members being transferred! BRC HQ at Vlotho decided the Section needed strengthening and appointed four ex-FAU members, one of whom, Ron Hodson is to be the new Section Leader. I have met them all at one time or another which is reassuring. Three women make up the team, Gladys, a teacher, who is deputy Section Leader, Gwen who is a nurse, and Joyce, a social worker. We have yet to arrange our areas of work, so everything is in a state of flux at the moment...

146 Relief Section, British Red Cross, c/o 117 RB Det. Mil. Gov., BAOR, 13 July 1946

We were just starting to get settled in when Ron, the Section Leader was taken into hospital with suspected TB, he had been working in refugee camps in the Ruhr. However, it turned out to be only a shadow and he is being allowed to return next week, but will have to take things easily. The work is on a rather larger scale than before. In Hannover we were attached to the Mil. Gov. Town Major working only in the city. Here we oversee a whole Regierungsbezirk *[region, similar to county]* which includes 15 Kreise *[local districts]* and we understand that both a Salvation Army and an FRS team also work in the area, but on specific projects. The area touches both the Russian and American Zones and extends from Göttingen and Hannoversch Münden in the south to Hildesheim and Peine in the north. A large, but a very nice part of the country to be in. At the moment I am involved with a nutritional survey of school children in Kreis Clausthal-Zellerfeld in the Harz mountains, with Dennis Berry, one of the ex-FAU members. At present the British Control Commission allows children in the larger cities to have a slightly higher food ration than those living in rural areas, on the assumption that those in the country can supplement their ration a little from locally grown produce. Kreis Zellerfeld has been designated as rural, but in fact the area is all mountains and forests and there is virtually no agriculture, so the food situation is similar to that in a city. During the war the area was considered safe from bombing and thousands of children were evacuated here. Some still do not know if they have families or homes to return to in the devastated towns, while the parents of others feel they are better off where they are, so for the moment it seems sensible to the authorities to keep the children here for the time being. On top of this many hundreds of homeless refugees came into the area after the war as it is so little damaged. So now the whole area has a population several times greater than it used to have. The object of our survey is to discover the extent of the malnutrition among the children and whether the area can be designated for the higher ration as in the towns. We realise we have to work quickly, as clearly time is important, but it is large area to cover and it will mean coming down here every day, and it is a sixty mile drive from Hildesheim *[in slow vehicles over very bad roads]*. Some

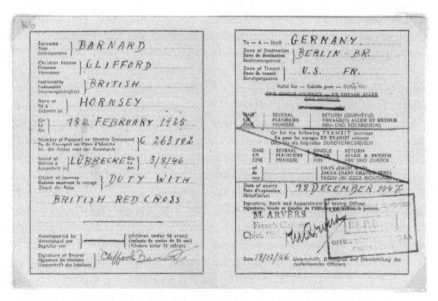

Military permit to enter British Zone in service with British Red Cross

compensation for us is the beautiful countryside, with winding roads and fresh mountain air. Before the war it was tourist area, but now the hotels and guest houses are full of refugees or used as homes for TB patients, etc...

146 Relief Section, British Red Cross, c/o 117 RB Det. Mil. Gov., BAOR, 20 July 1946

Many thanks for your letters. Glad to know Freda and John have moved in with you at '78' *[The family home. John had taken up work with the chemical company ICI in WGC.]* The food survey in Kreis Zellerfeld is still keeping me occupied. The plight of the refugees is quite dreadful... I managed to go into Hannover last Thursday evening. Renate and her family seemed quite well. They don't say anything but they must be feeling the latest cut in the food ration, now down to 1,050 calories a day. In the Section we now employ 10 local Germans – house staff, motor mechanics and so on – and give them all one meal a day from our ration strength, and we don't really notice it. It is the least we can do. *[This was not really permitted by the Control Commission for Germany (CCG).]* Renate gave me the enclosed letter she has written for you, Mummy. If it's in German I'm sure Daddy can translate it for you. She is very shy of her English, she understands very well, but speaks hesitantly. At the moment she is on holiday, but it is not certain when the Gymnastic School will re-open, as it is considered that the curriculum, which is naturally very physical, will use up too many calories. Neither the staff nor the students would have the strength to cope with a full term...

146 Relief Section, British Red Cross, c/o 117 RB Det. Mil. Gov., BAOR, 31 July 1946

Thank you for letting me know Owen *[Fountain, a WGC friend]* has left the Merchant Navy. I wonder what he will do know?... I have discovered I can renew my passport out here through the British Interests Branch of the Control Commission for Germany... Our survey of the food situation in Kreis Zellerfeld is now completed and Dennis *[Berry]* and I are hurriedly writing up our report for Mil. Gov. The statements from the local German bodies to augment our report had to be translated and incorporated into the whole. We have to take it to a Colonel, who we haven't met yet, and are hoping he will be sympathetic. Some Mil. Gov. people are only too glad to have our reports, but others think we are sticking our noses into their business... I enclose two photos Dennis took, one of me in the Harz on the Goslar–Clausthal road, you can see the wooded hills

Left: Clifford on the Goslar–Clausthal road. Below: Braunlager reservoir. Clifford's head is just visible between rails on the left.

(Dennis Berry)

behind. The other is of Braunlager reservoir which forms part of the border between the British and Russian Zones, both zones take water from the reservoir. We are standing at the head of the dam, which provides hydro-electricity. If you look closely you can just see my head in the bottom left-hand corner through the rails of the power house. I shall miss our visits to this lovely part...

146 Relief Section, British Red Cross, c/o 117 RB Det. Mil. Gov., BAOR, 14 August 1946

Mil. Gov. is still considering our food survey report. We put in a strong recommendation for school feeding, as the best way of tackling the problem. Now the whole team are involved in making surveys of all the Kreise in the Bezirk, trying to discover the main problems so we can know where to concentrate our efforts. The area is really far too large for one team, as we have to spend so much time in travel. We were still considering whether we should propose a second team for the area to HQ when we heard that there is a crisis situation in Schleswig-Holstein and could be moved up there, leaving no team at all here! We feel strongly opposed to this as there is clearly a real need here and to withdraw at this stage would really be letting the local German authorities down, and have put this view to HQ. We had understood that Schleswig-Holstein was one of the rather better off areas... Ron Hodson, the Section Leader, came back from hospital where he was being observed for TB, but has now contracted jaundice and is being sent to Denmark to convalesce and we are to have a new leader... Yes, Mummy, we eat well, although the food can be on the stodgy side. Renate has three apple trees in her garden and she gave me a whole lot to bring back to the Section which was well received... You ask about my pay. I get it when a woman comes round every so often. At the moment we aren't taxed, so from my weekly wage I get £2 put away for me in London, and £2.10s. for me to draw on here, which I can do whenever she visits. I gather some sort of interest is paid on the money one saves in London...

A rather older lady has joined the team, a Miss Laura Livingstone, who is on a special mission of some kind. She is the sister-in-law of the Bishop of Chichester, Dr Bell, who I expect you remember was outspoken about the saturation bombing of Germany during the war... I spent last weekend in Hannover with Renate and family. On Sunday we picked plums and apples in the garden and had them for supper. Langenhagen is not really a suburb of Hannover, but a small town in its own right, the trams from Hannover stop short, and the journey has to be completed by bus. The country around is rather flat with many cornfields, but not unpleasant, we went for a long walk the other evening. I enclose a letter from Renate for you, Mummy. She wants me to explain that she has written in German as she is not confident enough to put it English. Daddy will have to translate it for you. She is concerned how you may feel about me being friendly with a German girl. I have explained long ago that we are Quakers and about our attitude to war and reconciliation, but she is still a bit anxious about how British people may view Germans. My German is improving a bit. While I can understand most of what is said at mealtimes and so on, it is when I try to go into things more deeply that I get stuck, and frustratingly I find myself confined to short innocuous comments which sounds so inadequate. Why didn't I try harder at school!... While in Hannover I called in to see the old Section. David is still there but has been in hospital and is now going on leave. John Tanner has got engaged to Marianne, she appears in those snaps of us all on the river Aller, that I sent you *[pp. 124–25]*. He is expecting to return to England soon, as a medical student, he has got a place at Birmingham University. As he will be on a government grant he hopes it will be possible to get married next summer, and wants me to come to the wedding... I wonder if you could send me some of my civilian clothes. With so many soldier's wives and civilians attached to Mil. Gov. bodies about now, civvies are in fashion and it would be a relief to get out of khaki sometimes.

146 Relief Section, British Red Cross, c/o 117 RB Det. Mil. Gov., BAOR, 21 August 1946

Thanks so much for your letter to Renate, Mummy and the leaflets. I do appreciate your writing to her... We are all busy on our survey of the Bezirk and have not heard anything more about a possible move north. The head of the German Red Cross in Zellerfeld, Herr Junge, is very friendly towards me, and when I was discussing with him the work of his organisation in the area, I mentioned the possibility of another BRC team coming to the south of the Bezirk, his eyes lit up and asked if I would be in it and whether he should write to HQ and ask for me to be included! The fact that a school feeding scheme has now been started as a direct result of our report and discussions with Mil. Gov. has obviously raised his opinion of me. Both Herr Junge and the Oberkreisdirector couldn't thank us enough, they had been asking for a review of the child ration for three months. When I gave them the news they shook my hand very warmly and said, 'You have saved the lives of 5,000 children and we shall never forget this'. A little far fetched maybe, but I can understand their feelings. They wanted to show their gratitude and gave me and Dennis an open invitation to come on holiday in the Harz in better times at their expense, and made me promise not to forget. *[I'm sorry to say I never took the offer up]*... I received a parcel with a registered postmark from Stevenage, which contained coffee and stockings with an address in Osnabrück on a piece of card. There was no letter enclosed, but I assumed it had been sent to me to pass on. The only person I could think of in Stevenage who might have sent it was Mrs White, the solicitor's wife, who I seem to remember you once told me had relations in Germany. By a strange coincidence we had a visitor from Osnabrück, who turned out to know the recipient, Dr Marie Schiller, and was willing to take it to her. I enclosed my address so she can write to me when she receives it. I hope it was from Mrs White!

With Renate, Gisela and Elmar I had a lovely weekend at Elmar's parents house in Linden, in the west of Hannover across the river Leine, which divides the city. Herr and Frau Rössinger, Elmar's parents, were very pleased to see me and received the rations I had brought with a great show of pleasure, and immediately wanted to use the sugar and margarine to make a cake as it was Frau Rössinger's birthday on the Sunday. Herr Rössinger is a very nice man, with I discovered quite liberal attitudes and thought the war had been a disaster that should not have happened. He had been in the First World War and had had no liking for the Nazis. When Elmar's conscription arrived he made him join the Navy and got him into a Officer Training School at Kiel, which he considered to be the service least affected by Nazi thinking, and where at the end of the 1914–18 war the rebellion in the German Navy started. He was delighted when he discovered I had brought some English newspapers with me and spent the evening reading them, his English is not bad. I had also brought some pipe tobacco with me and offered it to him, his face glowed with pleasure and he went to a cabinet and took out a yellow cloth from which he produced a pipe which he showed me proudly. He had had it for over twenty years, but had put it away some years ago vowing never to smoke it again until he could get some proper tobacco. The present stuff, even if you can get it, is really poisonous, goodness knows what's in it. He filled his pipe and smoked contentedly, Frau Rössinger remarked she hadn't seen him so happy for years. On Sunday afternoon he insisted on playing chess with a lovely old set and board, and was surprised to discover I knew all the German names for the pieces and wanted to know the English equivalent. So all that coaching wasn't wasted, Daddy. The game was a long one but I managed to win in the end with a pawn made Queen. He insists on me coming again so he can have his revenge. On Saturday evening Renate and I had a long walk through parts of the city I had not seen before. I slept the night on a couch in Elmar's room, very comfortable. On Sunday evening, as it was Frau Rössinger's birthday we all went to a concert given by the Hannover Symphony Orchestra, conducted by Sergio Celibidache, we heard Mozart, Max Bruch, Tchaikovsky, Sibelius and Rimsky-Korsakov, a mixed bag but very enjoyable, only spoilt by the fact that I had to drive back to Hildesheim, to be ready for work on Monday morning, it takes over an hour so I wasn't in bed till after 1 am.

146 Relief Section, British Red Cross, Att.117 RB Det. Mil. Gov., BAOR, 30 August 1946

We have been told that the Section will be moved to Lübeck on the Baltic coast, and have been given two weeks to tie up our commitments here. The Section is not well pleased with this turn of events as we felt we were doing a good job here and don't want to let the local authorities down. The Colonel in charge of the Mil. Gov. Det. was also very reluctant to see us go and wrote to BRC HQ, and so did the Oberkreisdirektor in Zellerfeld, but BRC HQ were adamant, saying the need there is very desperate, so we shall see…

I had a strange and uncomfortable, but nevertheless interesting, encounter the other day. We met an ex-German Army officer *[why didn't I give his name and say where? It would have been of considerable interest now]* who we were given to understand had played a minor part in the plot to assassinate Hitler some months before the end of the war. Although he had been uncovered, he escaped execution but was sent to the Russian front. He had some unusual ideas, proposing that there should be a union of western countries and a crusade against Bolshevism. He had at the time of the war between China and Japan been a military attaché to General Chiang Kai-shek. He liked the Chinese saying they were a people who hated war and despised soldiers, yet he had come to realise that the situation in the world had gone so far that war, as terrible as it was, had become the only course open. He said that in the Soviet Union the Chinese saw a threat to the old cultures of the more experienced and tolerant nations – China in the east and Britain in the West. Will they defend themselves against the new, vigorous and dynamic life emanating from Russia, or will the British and Chinese empires crumble into decay, as the Roman Empire had done before them? And so he rambled on for over an hour, but I don't think any of us found him very convincing. When we at last got a word in to say we were pacifists, and took a rather different view of the world, he went very quiet and then asked if this was the new ideal of the youth of Britain? We had to point out that sadly our view was very much a minority one. This didn't cheer him but he must have been intrigued as he hoped we would visit him again and talk some more. Somehow I don't see any of us having that sort of time... Renate asked me to say that she was very pleased to have your letter and thinks you must be a very kind lady. She has started back at college and has a lot of work to do to prepare for some tests, but she will write again.

146 Relief Section, British Red Cross, Att. 117 RB Det. Mil. Gov., BAOR, 5 Sept. 1946

Still here in Hildesheim with no more news of a move. A member of the team went up to Lübeck to investigate, but Mil. Gov. had no knowledge of our proposed arrival, but confirmed that the situation is indeed desperate. Anyway it looks as if we shall be here a little longer and must make the best use of our remaining time... I received a letter from Frau Dr Schiller from Osnabrück thanking me for forwarding the parcel from Gertrude White. So my guess was right... We again spent the weekend with Elmar's parents and Herr Rössinger wanted to play chess again, but I won both games. I think he must be a bit rusty because I'm not a good player... People in the cities are now being allowed to draw their increased winter rations, 1,500 calories instead of 1,050, which is essential to say the least. The other great shortage is fuel; wood is unobtainable and electricity can only be used for lighting not heating and keeps being turned off. Gas is available for cooking but at a very low pressure. So people have to fend for themselves, which means there are no park benches and the like left, having been chopped up for firewood. Some electricity is available for industry. The Rössingers are very fortunate as their flat is part of a factory complex so when the electricity is switched on they can use it for heating... Renate was so pleased to have your letter, Daddy, especially as it was in German handwriting, and had to show it around...

146 Relief Section, British Red Cross, Att.117 RB Det. Mil. Gov., BAOR, 11 Sept. 1946

Still here but not for much longer. We move to Lübeck next Wednesday and have been busy packing up and saying our goodbyes to local German associates. Please don't send anything more here but I will let you have my new address when I know it. Two of the team are already there securing billets for us. We are sorry to leave, but understand a very big challenge awaits us. It is a bit of a way from Hannover, about three hours driving, but I hope I will be able to get there fortnightly or so, availability of transport and weather permitting. While I was in Hannover I looked in on the old Section. Martin Southwood is the only member left of the original FAU Section and there are now two or three American Quakers in the team working for the American Friends Service Committee. David Hughes is the Section Leader. Martin has had some good fortune. As he obtained unconditional exemption from military service at his tribunal he has been able to get a place to return to Oxford University to complete his studies, which will only be for a year. Then he will return to Germany where he has secured an assistant lectureship in English Literature at Göttingen University. He is amazing, when he came out here he literally could not speak a word of German and now he is very fluent, all self taught, he is obviously a natural linguist...

9. British Red Cross, Lübeck

September to December 1946

146 Relief Section, British Red Cross, att. 820 K Det. Mil. Gov., BAOR, 20 Sept. 1946

Safe and sound in Lübeck on the Baltic. A bit of a shambles settling in not quite up to FAU standard. We have quite a nice house although a bit on the small side for all of us. As there is no garage space and in view of all the pilfering at night we have to house the vehicles with a REME unit, but it is nearly a mile away, which is not too convenient. We hope it is only temporary as we are seeking our own lock up garage arrangements. Lübeck is a very old city, and has suffered some damage, but some old spires are still standing. I understand, however, that the Marienkirche, for example, is gutted inside and the bells which fell down during the bombing still lie on the floor. A number of shops seem to be open...

Robin *[Roberts]* (ex-FAU) has arranged for me and himself to play a game of football with a team from the Guards Brigade, if we measure up they may ask us to play again. I'm very much out of match practice, though...

146 Relief Section, British Red Cross, BAOR, 26 September 1946

Please note modified address, it omits the 'Mil.Gov.Det.' as we are registered direct with an Army Post Office (APO) located quite near us and so is convenient for picking up our mail ourselves. We are finding the accommodation is too small for us, and have no storage space at all, so we are actively looking for somewhere else. The Swedish Red Cross use a building which we think would be suitable and as they are looking to move we are hoping a deal can be arranged. It will have to be soon as we have 9 tons of stores waiting for us to collect from Hamburg docks. Our work is going to be concerned with the massive influx of refugees into the region who have been expelled from the areas of Germany ceded to Poland or fled from eastern Germany. We are still trying to size up the problems. We started by making contact with the German authorities

BRC Relief Section 146. Back row: Clifford, Robin Roberts (ex-FAU). Middle: Gwen (nurse), Frank Taylor (ex-FAU) in shadow, and Joyce (social worker). Front: Gladys Thomas (teacher) and Dennis Ward (team leader). Photo: Dennis Berry.

and opened an office in the German Red Cross building which is conveniently next door to the Jugendamt (Youth Office) and Fluchtlingsamt (Refugee Office). Lübeck is damaged but not to the extent of Hamburg, Bremen or even Hannover… The Guards Brigade, a very smart and efficient lot, are in charge of the region, which goes right up to the Russian Zone only five miles away.

We were due to play a game of football with the Scots Guards against an RASC *[Royal Army Service Corps]* side but it was called off as it rained all day and the ground was too sodden to play. It was played on Sunday afternoon instead. Although I enjoyed it I did not have a good game as I am sadly out of practice, and was stiff all over on Monday. Robin has been asked to play again but unsurprisingly I was not offered another game… Gertrude White sent me another parcel for Osnabrück. Last time you may remember I was able to have it delivered by hand, but as that was not possible this time I put it into the civilian post, which isn't really allowed. I have written to her and explained she would probably be better off in future sending it directly from England, although it might cost a bit more.

146 Relief Section, British Red Cross, BAOR 29 Sept. 1946

I had to borrow football boots and togs to play my last game, so as more games may be possible, could you send out my gear. Sorry to be a bother. Had a letter from John Tanner, he has started back at Medical School in Birmingham, buying books and so on. He hopes he can get Marianne over in about a year… I had to take two of the Red Cross women from the team to Hannover where they were going to catch a train for Berlin, so I had planned to spend the rest of the weekend with Renate. However, luck was against me. The car broke down on the autobahn south of Hamburg with an electrical fault which I was unable to fix. I stopped an Army truck who agreed to take the women and their baggage on to Hannover.

Then managed to hitch-hike a lift back to Hamburg where I telephoned the Section in Lübeck for a tow. Got another lift back to my stranded car and waited in the growing darkness. It was about 6 pm when the car broke down and past midnight before the truck from Lübeck reached me, with a smiling Frank *[Taylor]* and one of the German mechanics. I had just been preparing to spend the night in the car as a thick fog had descended, and I assumed they must have missed me. It didn't seem very wise to tow in the dark and fog, so we set about trying to fix the problem. I really could have done with a cup of tea! Eventually the mechanic got some life back into the engine and we got going. I had been seven hours on the autobahn and didn't tumble into bed till around 5 am. So much for my nice weekend in Hannover… Renate is back at school again, but Mil. Gov. have stipulated that the students have to take a 10 day break every month, although they can study their books at home. *[Was this I wonder to save heating costs or for the students' health?]*

Lübeck, I must say, is growing on me. It is a fine old seafaring port with a lot of character and some lovely old buildings. The newer parts of the city are well laid out – green, clean and little damaged. The main destruction was in the city centre, but even here there are now a few shops and cafes open. In the harbour a large number of fishing boats compete for space with the ships involved in the Baltic trade. The food situation is greatly helped by the plentiful supplies of fish. Strange that this doesn't seem to be the same in Hamburg which is only 45 miles away and where the food situation is one of the worst in the zone. But it is the refugee problem which overwhelms everything. The population of Lübeck and the surrounding area has doubled in a matter of months. Although compulsory billeting, with one family to a room, has housed many, there are still thousands trying to live in old and ill-repaired buildings or camps of hastily built wooden huts which have sprung up on bomb sites and other vacant plots, but the conditions are appalling. No electricity, fuel, running water, drainage or sewage, with ill-fitting windows without glass, just canvas and roofs which often leak. With little work many get involved in the black market and pilfering as a means of survival. The camps are both centres of infection and political unrest. Most were expelled from their homes in the 'New' Poland and parts of eastern Germany now occupied by Russian troops, with only what they could take with them. Underfed and robbed as they went, they have serious grievances and present a real fomenting problem for the British authorities.

The above letter gives only my view at the time, but during 2007 I read a very interesting and reflective article in The Guardian *of 30 June 1999* by Paul Oestreicher drawing attention to this massive and traumatic exodus, which we would now call 'ethnic cleansing'. As there was little sympathy for Germans it was barely reported, but at any other time would have made headline news. He wrote that some 10 million people were driven out of their homes, and of these some 2 million died on the freezing trek to the four Allied occupation zones (mainly the British and American, although some chose to remain in the Russian Zone and others went even further west to the French Zone.) In the Zones industry was laid waste, children were starving, and many thousands of houses were destroyed. In these pitiable conditions Germany had to absorb some 8 million displaced fellow Germans... For more than a generation the German expellees' organisations campaigned for the right to return to their homes. They and their children formed a significant part of the German electorate, but instead of giving way to this pressure Chancellor Willy Brandt went to Warsaw, knelt in penitence at the monument to the victims of Nazi terror, and negotiated a treaty which guaranteed Poland's western frontier. The German churches, in a historic document, had prepared the ground for this act of renunciation. With a dignified sense of reality, any claim on this historic German soil was abandoned. Since German unification, that has been solemnly reaffirmed.*

It also seems appropriate to mention here a long but very informative article, that appeared in The Guardian *during 1946, written by Richard Law, MP. As chairman of COBSRA he outlined some of the work being carried out, under their umbrella, by the multifarious groups from British*

* www.guardian.co.uk/theguardian/1999/jun/30/guardianweekly. guardianweekly1

voluntary societies. There were he said over 700 men and women, all vol-
unteers, in the British Zone of Germany trying to bring order out of chaos
and incidentally gaining for Britain the respect of a defeated and utterly
demoralized people. He felt the value of their work, scarcely appreciated
by their fellow countrymen at home, was difficult to over-estimate, bring-
ing to it, as they did, a devotion, a degree of practical common sense, and
an administrative capacity beyond praise.

The societies were called to Germany by the Army and retained by the
CCG for civilian relief and welfare work, providing a body of teams working
under official authority but preserving the spirit and much of the freedom of
unofficial enterprise. He remarked on their extraordinary achievement in
subordinating their cherished and ideological idiosyncrasies which might
so easily have weakened their effectiveness, due partly he believed to
the careful preparation which preceded their entry into Europe. Hundreds
of tons of food, used clothing and medical supplies had been distributed
since the middle of 1945, but their unique contribution has been their
capacity to stimulate German welfare organisations to face present prob-
lems, to inspire the Germans themselves to accept some responsibility for
their own future and to discover and meet needs of which CCG was una-
ware. After brief descriptions of many of the imaginative projects he wrote
of the 'steady gallantry of those who labour uncomplainingly in the stench
and filth and misery of the refugee camps of Schleswig-Holstein'. As the
only team in the area it must have been a reference to our work in Lübeck.

146 Relief Section, British Red Cross, BAOR 7 October 1946

Thanks for sending on the two letters, one was from John Tanner, now
studying medicine in Birmingham, and the other from Gordon Taylor
who is leading a building scheme for FAU Post War Service in France.
Nice to hear from them and to keep in touch... No football game this
weekend so drove to Hannover, about three hours. They were very
pleased to see me but are finding this sudden cold very hard as they have
no heating at all! The recent calorie rise in the food ration is very much
appreciated, but in reality it is a dire necessity.

It may just be the onset of winter but the work is beginning to get
me down and I find I am tending to do things rather mechanically. I'm
so tired of seeing all this bomb damage, miserable people in worn out
clothes many with yellow starved faces, stinking run down camps and
so on. It is such a stupid world! It concerns me too that I find I am getting short on sympathy and compassion and would so like to return to
normality, but what is normality? I don't yet know what awaits me when

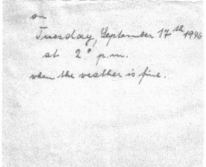

Invitation to a children's party, German Red Cross, Clausthal

I return to England. However, I realise I have to stay on here to work out my time and must just make the most of things. I am so lucky to have a home to return to with loving parents, and of course there are other considerations here!... An Army dentist has set up in the next street to us so I thought I should pay him a visit, only one small hole to fill, not bad after at least two years... I thought you might like to see the little invitation card I received to a children's party at the German Red Cross Kindergarten in Clausthal. They must have appreciated my time there when I was working on the school feeding scheme, but I had already left Hildesheim, so it wasn't possible for me to go, but it warmed my heart at just the right time, and helped make things worthwhile.

146 Relief Section, British Red Cross, BAOR 15 October 1946

I'm sorry to have sounded so depressed in my last letter and should have realised you would start worrying. There is no need, I'm fine. I wrote in the evening after a tiring day and let out some negative feelings. Of course, I would like to come home now and get on with the next phase of my life, but I have to fulfil the conditions of my tribunal and there is terrible need here. All the predictions are that conditions in Europe will start to improve slowly from next Spring and that the road to recovery can be seen, which will make things a lot more bearable. At least I am earning a little money now and from Christmas I can renew my contract with the BRC from month to month, although in practice, I gather, only a week's notice is required. Most important of all, being here means I can see Renate from time to time, which would be impossible if I returned to England. As you will have guessed by now from my letters Renate and I are getting very fond of each other, in fact I'm sure she is the girl for me! We have to work out all the implications of this, but one thing we have is time, so we shall certainly not do anything hastily. If I get Christmas leave I will tell you our plans to date... I haven't been able to visit your Dr Neumann yet, but I have it in mind and when I next go to Eutin, it is only about 20 miles further north from there, I will call in. I did have to go to Kiel a few days ago which is even further on. My first visit, it seemed to be very heavily damaged, and there were many hulks of half sunk ships lying there. The drive was pleasant through little hills and lakes. I have heard it referred to as the 'Kleine Schweiz'.

Last Sunday although sunny was not that warm, but all the same four of us decided to visit Niendorf, a pretty little fishing village not far from Travemünde. We hired a boat and rowed out in the bay, it was a bit choppy with white flecked waves and it was hard going compared to rowing on a river. I kept finding the oar in the air not the water, but it was good fun and now I have been on the Baltic Sea! Niendorf harbour was packed with fishing boats of all shapes and sizes, intriguing to watch them squeeze between the walls of the narrow harbour entrance. They fish off the Danish coast, and also at either end of the Kattegat and Skagerrak where apparently large shoals of fish gather, but sometimes go further north to the Norwegian coast... Very interested to hear Freda and John's news about the house they are having built, I wonder what it will be like?

146 Relief Section, British Red Cross, BAOR 24 October 1946

I am writing this in our office. We have two rooms in the German Red Cross building which is reasonably warm as they have fuel to burn. I spend a fair amount of time here as there seems to be more and more paper work these days, mainly forms to fill in and letters, reports and indents to do with supplies and so on, far more red tape than there used to be. The building is right in the centre of town on a corner of one of the main streets, so we have traffic noise all day. Opposite is Lübeck's 'covent garden' and I can see the lorries going in and out laden with vegetables, one wouldn't think there was a food shortage, but with a population of around 300,000, I suppose its not so much...

146 Relief Section, British Red Cross, BAOR 30 October 1946

Thank you for your letters and for being so understanding about my wishing to stay out here for the time being. I should be getting some leave around Christmas, depending on the personnel strength of the team, so we can talk some more then... Fascinating to hear about Jack Peel's meeting with Stalin, I wonder what impressions he gained? *[Jack Peel, a friend of my father who lived in WGC, was a fluent Russian speaker. He*

145

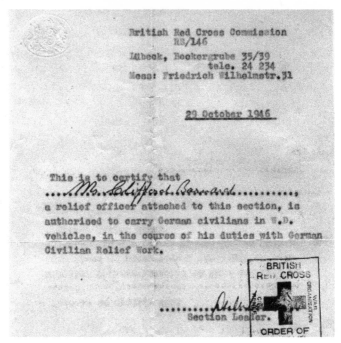

Permit to carry German civilians

had served as an interpreter with the RAF Wing on the Russian front during the war and was occasionally called upon to accompany British groups meeting government officials]... The letter you forwarded was from Gaydu. I haven't heard from him for months. He is still in Italy but hasn't had home leave for over a year, which is a bit rough... Another parcel of clothing from Denis Roberts. I wrote to thank him, saying that, of course, we can use anything he sends, but that it might be better to send it through the channels which have been set up to specialise in the distribution of clothing. I couldn't undertake to dispense the items individually myself, so I put the parcel with other supplies going to German voluntary organisations destined for refugee camps, as they know where the need is greatest. The latest reckoning is that there are 15,000 refugees in camp sites and another 60,000 billeted in people's houses in the Stadtkreis of Lübeck alone... Last weekend I had an unexpected trip to Hannover with Frank *[Taylor]*. When the team left Hildesheim we had to leave one of our trucks behind for repair and it was subsequently taken to some workshops in Brunswick, and could now be collected. We left about 4.30 am and drove to Brunswick where we deposited a spare part to be fitted that had been delivered by mistake directly to us in Lübeck. From there we drove to

Hannover to see David Curtis and Section 2, but now all different people. Then on to Renate's where I had arranged we could stay the weekend.

Elmar was to be there as well. By the way Elmar has a distant relative, in Hurlingham, London, who is the medical superintendent of a hospital, he would like me to take something to him when I am next on leave. They were all well but feeling the cold as they still have no fuel, so we sat in the kitchen with blankets around us, rather cosy. They take it all in good part laughing and smiling all the time. The higher food ration is helping but hardly compensates for the lack of fuel. Gas and electricity is severely rationed and there is a rush to make a hot drink when it comes on. On Saturday we all went to an art exhibition in Hannover, there were some interesting things – pottery, jewellery, wooden items, woven carpets, and much else. On the Monday morning Frank and I drove to Brunswick to pick up the repaired truck before returning to Lübeck... I have had a tip off and am going to see the British staff officer at a Kriegsmarine arsenal to see if I can get some surplus stocks released – bedding, furniture, etc., for the refugee camps, then also to a Mil.Gov. Army Salvage depot on the same mission... Tonight, Gladys wants me to go with her to the Anglo-German club she has started, we mainly discuss current affairs, many thinking Germans are eager to do this in a free and open way.

146 Relief Section, British Red Cross, BAOR
3 November 1946

No real news at present. Played football in the rain yesterday, for the Irish Guards against the 10th Hussars, who won 3-0! Very unfortunately Robin, who was also playing, received a bad kick and is now in hospital with a suspected broken ankle. He is very fed up as he was due to go on home leave. Nothing decided about my home leave yet, but I'm due for a 72 hours which I can add to the Christmas break, so I may use it to go to Hannover... Would you tell Freda that we have been asked not to take on individual cases as we used to do, so it's a bit difficult for me to visit this Frau Neumann for Methyr Fox, she would do better to direct her request to the Foreign Relations Branch of the Red Cross, who now have a network of specially trained people over here to handle these cases. Denis Roberts is still sending me parcels of clothing, so I have written and told him that I can't distribute the items individually myself, but that they go to a central store which allocates them in rotation to every camp. Any food items are given to the camp clinics to give to their neediest cases... Would it be possible for you to buy a toothbrush for Renate, you can't get them here. I assume they are still available in England?

146 Relief Section, British Red Cross, BAOR
10 November 1946

Had a bit of a temperature on Tuesday and spent the day in bed, got up on Wednesday but spent the day in the house, felt a good deal better on Friday and went into the office to tackle the paper work. Gwen, who is an SRN and a motherly type, keeps an eye on us when we are not feeling so good. Her main work is liaising with the German public health authorities, visiting hospitals and reporting on nurse training and so on...Very interested to have Jack Peel's impressions of Moscow, it's so difficult to get any reliable information from behind the 'iron curtain', and there are so many rumours around... Thanks for the *News Chronicle* with the New Year's demob. programme. I note they are some three months behind what was forecast earlier. This would make my release about August. I can't complain, even then I will only have done 4 years, whereas those in the forces who were in at the beginning will have done 5 or even 6 years. There are some good points about a slower demob. I have read that American forces have been released far too quickly before any proper preparations have been made and no jobs to go to... Yesterday we moved into a larger house which can accommodate the ten of us much better. The main drawback is that the only means of heating water is a gas geyser in the bathroom. I defy anyone to get a hot bath from a gas geyser! There are continental style stoves in the living and dining rooms but our coal ration is hardly adequate... There are rumours, I sincerely hope unfounded, that the food ration for the German population will be cut, this would be devastating on morale, which was just showing signs of picking up a little. One has the feeling that there could be more co-operation between the zones. The Russian has large food growing areas but little heavy industry, couldn't steel be sent from the British zone in exchange for food, for example? Maybe there are plans for this, but nothing apparent. We have heard that British troops in the Ruhr have been put on the alert to deal with possible food riots. The latest joke is the nickname for the Control Commission for Germany (CCG) – 'Complete Chaos Germany'– not really fair I think.

146 Relief Section, British Red Cross, BAOR
24 November 1946

Many thanks for parcels, newspapers and letters, they really are appreciated. Unfortunately, there was a minor mishap in one parcel, as it got bashed in transit and the cocoa had spilt out, but I managed to salvage most of it. Can unknitted wool be washed? It is cocoa colour now. Yes, of course, I will send on a coffee parcel to Herr Link, but you know the internal parcel post is not all that reliable. I read in the papers that in reply to a question in the House of Commons it was hoped to lift the ban on food parcels from Britain to Germany soon. Alternatively, Reg Middleton, who works in the American Zone often visits Munich, I could write and ask him if could deliver it... By the way Mil.Gov. have told me they have no objection to the translation of Wallace's letter into German *[Henry Wallace, vice-president under Franklin D. Roosevelt and later as Secretary of Commerce. He unsuccessfully stood for President in 1948]*, but cannot sanction its printing because of the paper shortage. They would, however, be happy for us to place a typewritten copy in the reading room of the central library. Something, I suppose... Many thanks for the toothbrush for Renate, can I have one too? I will settle up when I get home. Thank Freda for her letter, I'm sorry to hear about the delays to the building of their house. It's so kind of you to think of knitting Renate a pair of woollen gloves... The section is trying to work out a leave rota; I could leave just after Christmas and be home on New Year's Day, not definite as the 'manpower' situation is still unclear as two team members cannot be away for more than a week at the same time... My watch has broken down again. I took it to a German watch repairer who said it needed a new balancer, which he can't get, although he would be willing to do the repair if I can get one. I will bring it home with me.

146 Relief Section, British Red Cross, BAOR
1 December 1946

I am enclosing Reg's address so you can send Herr Link's coffee parcel direct, for him to deliver. I have written to him. Also Renate's address as you asked for it... I went to a 'Stars in Battledress' performance of Emlyn Williams' *Night Must Fall*, really very good amateur production... As you know part of our job is to try and obtain anything which might help to improve the conditions of refugees and we have at long last been given a pass which allows us to go into any depot or factory stores which is under the control of the CCG. It means a member of the team can go and look around and see if we can find anything suitable and then indent for CCG for its release. We have managed to find 800 ex-army beds in varying state of repair. It may sound a good number, but 50,000 might be nearer the mark. Although we got them released we couldn't find the means to transport them. Mil. Gov. offered one railway wagon on a train, which might run in about three weeks time. Then we found a local German firm with three lorries who said they could do the job, but couldn't say when. We shall just have to wait, but even when we get them we have to find a way of getting the individual beds to the dozens of places where they are needed...

146 Relief Section, British Red Cross, BAOR
15 December 1946

It's Sunday morning and the church bells are ringing. Cold and white with snow and our vehicles parked outside are just covered mounds. From our sitting room window we can just see a canal which is frozen over and people are already skating on it, where do they find the energy on their rations? Two small children have just passed, well wrapped up with woollen caps, pulling a sledge along with a large Christmas tree on it. One thing which isn't rationed is Christmas trees, but otherwise it's not going to be much of a Christmas for people. I came back from a present buying trip empty-handed. Those shops which are open are doing their best to decorate with fir branches and cones, but there was little to buy, only wooden knick-knacks, model wooden ships and a few toys. Advent is marked with wreaths and candles, parties and carol singing, and St Nicholas for the children on the 6th. Several British Army units are giving parties for children and Mil. Gov. is laying on a party for 500 refugee children. It is heart warming and being reciprocated. At a rehabilitation centre for limbless German soldiers, I found many had been making wooden toys. A group there wished to send a sack to children who had been bombed out in London. With such an expression of good will I went off to Mil.Gov. to see how it might be arranged, but I was told it was quite impossible with mumbles about export permission and transport at a time of great shortages, etc. All just excuses I felt and was so deflated... My leave is still on and I should be home soon after Jan 1st. This time I have to go via the Cuxhaven–Hull route, which I haven't done before, it should be interesting.

A six week gap which included two weeks home leave.

10. British Red Cross, Lübeck and Hannover

January to July 1947

146 Relief Section, British Red Cross, BAOR
23 January 1947

Here I am back with the Section just in time for dinner today. We got to Hull about 1 pm, were given a meal and then embarked, sailing about 3 pm. To start with the crossing was quite smooth but later a wind got up and the sea became quite choppy, but I managed some breakfast, and it became smoother as we approached Cuxhaven, as the sea was frozen over and ice breakers were at work. We spent the night in a transit hotel and left by train to Lübeck at 4.15 am! It's considerably colder here than in England...

146 Relief Section, British Red Cross, BAOR
2 February 1947

Still very cold. I've written to Hannah Leather explaining I can't visit her friends until the weather improves... So sorry to hear you have been unwell, Mummy. I've had a bit of a cold myself, but it seems to be getting better now. Snow covers everywhere, it is powdery and the wind blows it up in clouds. The canals and harbour are deeply frozen. I went to Hannover last weekend, they are reasonably well and have a bit more heating. I also visited the Rössingers to tell them of my visit to their relatives in Hurlingham, when I was on leave. However, when I came to leave the truck wouldn't start, so had to beg a tow from a nearby Army unit and tried to start it that way, but I hadn't realised it was very low on oil and the engine seized up. I had no option but to leave it in an Army workshop and go back to Langenhagen for the night. The following morning I tried to get a train to Hamburg, but I had no travel permit and had to visit David Curtis in the Red Cross office at Mil. Gov. to write me out a pass. The first train I could catch was not until 5 pm and it was past 8 pm before I phoned the Section to ask to be picked up.

However, no-one wanted to turn out and drive to Hamburg in the dark and on frozen roads, so I had to spend the night in the Officers' hotel and travel back the next day with a truck which came to collect stores. I was not back with the Section till Tuesday evening and the Section Leader and Transport Officer were none too pleased to say the least, particularly as somebody from HQ visited on Monday and wanted to know where I was! I felt sorry to have made it so awkward for the Section Leader. Nothing to do with this incident but my work has been changed and I have taken over the inspection of refugee camps and sites in Kreis Eutin, an area north of Lübeck. I will take an official from the Kreis Flüchtlings-versorger (Refugee Care) on my visits. She is a Canadian lady, a fluent German speaker, who married a German man and has lived here during the war. He is still a prisoner in Russia. Life is very, very difficult for these refugees and the reports we will have to make to the local authorities are not going to be easy…

My inspection of refugee sites in Kreis Eutin occasionally took me through Scharbeutz on the coast, from where I could see the upturned hull of a large ship out in the bay. My enquiries revealed a terrible tragedy. The political prisoners in Sandbostel had been transferred under horrific con-ditions from a larger concentration camp, Neuengamme, near Hamburg, but many were kept in this camp but fared no better. With the Allied armies approaching from west, east and south, thousands were transported northwards and put aboard three ships in Lübeck Bay. It is not clear what the ultimate intention was. Unfortunately, the RAF, mistaking the ships for military transports, bombed and sank all three on 3 May 1945, only two days before the 'cease fire' and the end of hostilities. There were very few survivors. The incident is considered among the worst maritime disasters of the twentieth century, far surpassing, for example, the sinking of the Titanic, *when some 1,500 people were lost. On the largest ship, the* Cap Arcona, *4,650 drowned, on the* Thielbeck *another 2,750 and further hun-dreds on the third boat. (Source: National Maritime Museum)*

146 Relief Section, British Red Cross, BAOR
9 February 1947

It is so cold, one only has to put a head outside and it takes your breath away. I'm told the temperature dropped to –20°C during Friday, the cold-est day recorded in Lübeck since 1928. Is that kind of temperature pos-sible here? Everywhere, is of course, frozen solid, including the ships in the harbour, and a fishing fleet out in the Baltic Sea which is unable to move, so the RAF have been dropping food to them. Transport is badly affected and Army cinemas and clubs closed as they can't be heated, and I understand, even some billets. At the moment we have coal for about three weeks, but are restricting bath nights to two a week, there are seven in the team at the moment. The rations come in alright, but are rather dull, no fresh potatoes only powdered stuff, and so on, but we really can't complain, as it is so much worse for the local populace... I have started on my tour of inspection of refugee sites in Kreis Eutin, which is probably half the size of Hertfordshire, some 20 miles north of Lübeck. It is harrowing. Many people are trying to eke out an existence in any building that they could find at the time of the enormous influx following the mass expulsion from the eastern areas. Too many are in a bad state of repair and quite unsuitable for people to live in. For example, I found two families sharing a disused petrol station. Many are still in wooden huts or sheds, which had been hastily erected on bombed sites or plots of waste ground. Mostly without electricity, piped water, sewage facilities, little fuel, and no glass in the windows, just covered with a canvas material. Fortunately, there don't seem to be any people still in tents. Few men have paid work and spend their time scrounging or involved in the black market. I am told there is a street market where if you have anything stolen you can usually find it on one of the stalls to buy back! One family of four had only one blanket under which they all slept together. The schools are shut as there is no heating, so children tend to stay in bed all day to keep warm, in any case few have serviceable shoes and warm clothes to go out. Happily, I could find no obvious signs of any epidemics yet. CCG released to us 1,000 ground sheets, which we had indented for three months ago, but could do with many more, although blankets would be more appropriate now...

Frank is investigating special entrance exams for service men for executive posts in the Civil Service. He has shown me the literature he has received and it seems quite interesting, so I'm writing off for the papers for myself... We now have a wireless and can listen to the news as it happens instead of hearing everything two days after it has occurrred, and of course, listen to concerts and the like. BFN (British Forces Network) reception is good and some of the programmes interesting...

146 Relief Section, British Red Cross, BAOR
16 February 1947

Very many thanks for the parcels and cards. I'll take Renate's to her when I go down next weekend. Knowing there was a cake in my parcel and fearing it might go stale, I brought it down for Sunday tea. Everyone said it was delicious and Mrs Mood, an older member of the team, said you must have been saving up all your sugar ration! It was so kind of you all... The big news is that demob is to be speeded up. It has been posted up in all Army unit orders last Thursday and as you might expect it is the major talking point among the troops. Group 53 will be out by 8 July and my group 52 will be out by 25 June, as you know conchies are released 2 or 3 weeks after the last servicemen in their group has gone, so that means I could be home in July, some 3 months earlier than I anticipated. A Colonel from Red Cross HQ has been visiting all the Sections to inform them that it is intended to reduce the overall personnel from 200 to 100. Although a timetable for this has not yet been drawn up, he wanted to know what individual intentions would be in the light of this. *[I can't recall any reasons being given for this reduction, but assume it was financial, or lack of volunteers, as the need was still as great]*... The Section Leader arranged for all of us to have a chest X-ray at the Stadtkrankenhaus, where we are known to the Medical Superintendent. He said he was very glad to do this for us as we had been so generous in giving supplies to the hospital. We were all o.k.... One of the letters you sent on to me was from the Rössingers' relatives in Hurlingham whom I visited when I was on leave at Christmas, thanking me and hoping I will visit again. The mother has now arrived from Germany to live with them, they had been trying for months to get her over... Sorry to hear there is so little progress on Freda's house.

146 Relief Section, British Red Cross, BAOR 2 March 1947

Time seems to be flying past at the moment. I went to Renate's for the weekend and gave her the watch. She likes it very much and said she didn't know what to say, wearing it all the time and constantly looking at it. She also loved the brooch and is writing to you. Thank you for the parcels with all the things for our birthdays, I do really appreciate it... There is still a great deal of snow on the roads and driving was slow and difficult. When I came to leave I found the headlamps from my vehicle had been stolen. I park it round the back of the school building which we hoped would be out of sight, evidently not. As it was already dark it was not possible for me to drive back that night and had to wait until morning. The Section Leader was very annoyed as he saw it as some misdemeanour, although it was hardly of my own making, but clearly it's not going to be so easy to get permission to go to Hannover over a weekend in future.... I've been going to my area in Eutin several days a week now, but the driving is difficult as several of the minor roads are still closed by snow drifts and others down to one lane. It seems to be getting a little milder so maybe a thaw is on the way at last... The HQ Personnel Officer visited us again to update us on the planned reduction. The intention is now to cut each team down to about six people, but as it won't be immediate he thought it would be alright for me to stay till July. He certainly didn't want to lose any of us ex-FAU and would prefer to move us to another Section rather than send us home. I hope it doesn't come to this, but I would accept a transfer rather than come back to England. After discussing the situation with each member of the team individually he insisted in taking us all to the Officers' Country Club at Travemünde for supper. It is the first time I have been there and the luxury rather shook me. We had a drink at the bar beforehand and I was staggered to see egg after egg, which are supposed to be in such short supply, being used to make dozens of brandy flips and the like, what the German barman thought of this I can only imagine. Supper was soup, fish, roast chicken, a dessert, and finally coffee, washed down with white wine, all for 9 shillings each. I believe all the food is brought in from Denmark, nevertheless it does seem rather callous when the local populace are so hard put to feed themselves. Apparently, at weekends the place operates all night long with dance music and cabaret shows finishing with bacon and eggs at 6 am! I can imagine this is how the British Raj behaved in India. Then last night we had a party for Mrs Mood, who is leaving, with about 30 guests both German and British. It was a bit of a squash but we got them all into our sitting and dining rooms. Someone had managed to rustle up quite a reasonable buffet and good time was had…

146 Relief Section, British Red Cross, BAOR 9 March 1947

The week started with a thaw and just as we thought it would continue it started snowing all over again. The roads are as bad as ever and I have not been able to get to Eutin, so have spent most of the time in the office. You ask how the general situation is now and I can only say that it is very difficult to see any significant change, although the statistics say there has been some improvement. The severe weather has slowed coal production which in turn affects industry, and transport has been much hampered. Hearsay has it that in many parts of the country the food ration of 1,500 calories is not being met, although I haven't had any reports of that here in Schleswig-Holstein. In Hannover bread was unobtainable for several days running. I don't know how it is in the Ruhr, but it is generally accepted as being the worst hit area. One statistic that is worse is the death rate for old people, presumably from the severe weather and winter illnesses… I quite enjoy working in Kreis Eutin, when I do get there, it must be lovely in the summer as the whole coastline is made up of holiday resorts. At the moment, of course, the hotels and guest houses are crammed with refugees and even the little huts on the beaches. The sea is still frozen over and icebreakers are being used in the harbour. Scroungers have been scrambling over the ice to get out to frozen ships laden with coal and been helping themselves, this is a dangerous thing to do so they must be very desperate... Today the sun is shining and the birds are singing, but I think they must be missing Mrs Mood as she was always feeding them with crumbs in the morning.

146 Relief Section, British Red Cross, BAOR 16 March 1947
Weather a bit warmer with a slight thaw during the day creating slush and flooding, which then freezes at night which has meant we have had to put chains on our vehicles, such a bind fixing them on... Interested to hear you met Anthony Harris's mother and to learn he is already demobbed. I believe those in the Navy have been released more quickly than the Army. I wonder where he is going to study mining engineering. The letter you forwarded from Hatfield was from the local branch of the Red Cross who hope I will join them when I return and give a talk about my work... Renate is better now but has not returned to college as the trams have stopped running; she doesn't feel up to the 4 mile walk yet.

146 Relief Section, British Red Cross, BAOR 30 March 1947
With the better weather I have been able to get out every day, but it is rather tiring driving around visiting and inspecting places and meeting people all with needs, mostly way beyond my ability to rectify, but the lady who comes with me keeps the local authorities well informed on what we find... I got to Hannover last weekend and found Renate well and we had a long walk in the countryside on Sunday morning, but I had to leave around 4 pm for the drive back. I hope to go again over Easter when I have the extra day... I have received more information from the Civil Service, but I understand that as I am not in HM Forces I am no longer eligible for the reconstruction competitions as the date for civilians is passed.

However, I did receive a letter which suggested that as I had done full time alternative service they may be able to use the discretion allowed them in my favour. So I have filled up all the forms and sent them back, and I have received notification that my case is being considered. I don't know where the exams are held. The exam papers don't look too bad, except the Maths, I'll have to do some swotting, the others are on English language and an essay, also general knowledge and general intelligence. Out of 900 marks the interview carries 300 and the papers 100 each. The salaries look good to me, I suppose I might find something in the Ministry of Health, anyway I will have to wait and see at least it is another possible option... Could you send me some more vitamin C tabs as I have run out, our rations are so stodgy, still no potatoes and only three loaves for the nine of us for three days, no jam and very little sugar, but adequate butter and cheese, the vegetables have all obviously got frozen at some point. Mustn't complain as the food situation is far worse for the German people. There have been strikes in the Ruhr, but the suggestion in the newspapers that these are politically motivated is ludicrous, they are just plain hungry, and find it difficult to work with so little food. Here there are long bread queues from morning to evening, people arrive before the baker starts and virtually grab the loaves as they come out of the ovens.

146 Relief Section, British Red Cross, BAOR 10 April 1947

I had a wonderful Easter in Hannover, but it was rather a roundabout journey as I took a Red Cross nurse to Bad Rehburg and a German interpreter to Rotenburg, and collected them on the way back. It was not without incident either. On the way there we passed an accident and as we had an ambulance we stopped and offered assistance, which ended in us taking a man to hospital with a suspected broken leg. On the return I thought by leaving at 4 pm I would have plenty of time, but owing to heavy rain I got stuck in mud on a minor road and had to walk some two miles to an army airstrip to ask for a tow out. Then I realised I was running low on petrol and thought I had better try and find an army depot where I could fill up. The first place I tried was closed for the holiday; eventually I was successful but did not get back to Lübeck till around 1.30 am! It was good though to have the long stay from Friday to Monday. On the Sunday David Curtis and Marianne *[John Tanner's girlfriend]* came to tea and we all had a catching up time. There was an egg for all of us which had been coloured in the traditional way and we learned about the 'Osterhase', when coloured or chocolate eggs are hidden for the children to find, rather like a 'hunt the thimble game'. I don't suppose many German families will be playing the game this year. As we expected there have been reports of hunger strikes so it would appear that the German people are not going to accept the situation without protest. I suppose they feel it could get worse and have to act now before they get any weaker. Despite previous CCG promises, Hynd *[head of British Control Commission]* has now admitted that the 1,500 calorie ration is rarely being met, more usually 1,000 to 1,300 varying from area to area. The economic situation has to be improved during the coming summer months. It is estimated that some 30% of the food produced finds its way onto the black market, partly due, I suppose, because there is so little trust in the value of the Mark. The agreement between the American and British Zones does not seem to be working very well; goods from the British Zone are getting into the American but little of the promised food is being sent in return. The position is very well put by Victor Gollancz in a letter to *The Times* on April 5. *[This letter, I believe, marked the beginning of his Save Europe Now campaign].* I can see that Germany has to be an economic whole for things to work, but this has to include the Russian Zone and at present that seems to be an impossibility. Meanwhile reparations are still being taken, particularly in the Russian and French sectors – railway lines being ripped up, telegraph wires pulled down and factories dismantled, which must be setting Germany's recovery back many years. If these countries really have to take these reparations, surely it would be better to wait a few years until Germany industry has been re-established when worthwhile goods can be provided, but I suppose Russia, which was so devastated, is in need right now, and probably France too.

An overall economic policy and a new currency need to be agreed by the occupying powers as an urgent necessity. I gather the strikes on the whole were more token demonstrations, although a few people were injured and British Army vehicles set on fire in Brunswick, Hamburg and the Ruhr towns, where a press photographer was pulled out of his car, his camera smashed and his car pushed into a river. I expect these were the usual wilder elements that latch onto these occasions. It was mostly quieter in Hannover and also Lübeck, where the march was orderly and a crowd gathered outside the Rathaus. The Bürgermeister received a deputation, and water and electricity switched off for an hour. British troops helped the German police control the crowds. Dennis Ward, our Section Leader, managed to take some snaps of the marches. One poster slogan read, 'We don't want calories but something to eat' in English... I am doing what I can in Eutin but it is little enough, although I did have a letter from Colonel Jones thanking me for taking an interest in his Kreis, which made me I feel a shade better.

146 Relief Section, British Red Cross, BAOR 18 April 1947

Great news about Daddy's possible visit here for the CCG, let me know when you have the details, as I'm sure we can arrange to meet up. Maybe, Renate too. I enclose all the telephone numbers so you can get in touch once you have arrived.

My father, Cyril Barnard, accepted an invitation from the British Control Commission to join a team of investigators, all specialist librarians, to visit in the British Zone of Occupied Germany from 18 May to 2 June to make a study of mechanical aids to documentation and systems of classification. While he was in Germany I was able to take him to visit Renate and her family in Langenhagen.

146 Relief Section, British Red Cross, BAOR 22 April 1947

Any more news of Daddy's trip here? Lovely weather at the moment, although we have had a few thunderstorms. It is beautiful country around Eutin, all lakes and little hills, and it is at its best in the sunshine... Thanks for the offer to get some specimen question papers for the reconstruction competitions for recruitment to the executive classes of the civil service... Off to play a game of soccer this afternoon.

146 Relief Section, British Red Cross, BAOR 27 April 1947

Many thanks for all your letters and packets. I have forwarded Freda's to Renate and Mummy's to Frau Schmalgemeyer *[Renate's mother]*. Weather good although we have had a few gales. Football game on Tuesday evening with an Army side against a German team, it was a 3-3 draw, exhausting but good fun... No signs of an easing in the food crisis, bread could be in even shorter supply... I'm due for some short leave soon. Robin *[Roberts]* and Frank *[Taylor]* are going to Switzerland before going home, so I'm going to see if I can wangle 10 days in Hannover. This may seem a bit silly as I shall be home for good in about three months, but could you send a few of my civvies; just trousers and a shirt. In this warmer weather everyone changes into civvies for the weekends, except the regular soldiers. I can send them home in a parcel before I finally leave.

146 Relief Section, British Red Cross, BAOR 7 May 1947

Time is flying by with so much happening. The Section is even smaller at the moment with two leaving for home and one on leave in Switzerland. The reduction means there is a bit of a strain and in addition I have been asked to help out at HQ in Vlotho for three weeks in June, while people are on leave. This could well be my last job here. I would return to the Section before taking a last few days in Hannover, I hope, then packing and returning to England which now looks like being in July... Managed to get hold of some films so we took some snaps last weekend, I've now got quite a few to show you. Took your two wonderful parcels with me. I can't describe how excited and pleased they all were. Thank you very much it is so kind of you and means a great deal to me... Waiting eagerly for Daddy's visit, over Whitsun I presume now.

146 Relief Section, British Red Cross, BAOR 14 May 1947

Very many thanks for parcels and letters. Renate loves the shoes and will be writing to you when she is off school on Thursday. She doesn't get much spare time as she is up at six every morning and is often not home until 8 pm, travelling on the buses and trams is very tiring and feeling hungry all the time. Driving through Hamburg on my way to Hannover the air was thick with dust from all the heaps of rubble, so dense at times that it affects one's breathing, everywhere is covered in thick layers. It must be awful for people who have to live in this atmosphere the whole time, I was glad to get into the countryside again... I took Renate to see the film *Great Expectations*, she understood the whole plot and far more of the dialogue than I thought she would. We must do it more often if we can. Sunday we just lazed in the sun. On Monday I went on to Vlotho to see the Transport Officer, who I will be replacing temporarily during the reduction period from June 6th, to discover what I shall have to do... Most of our transport is in workshops at the moment so I can't get out for a bit, hence this letter... I'm not surprised to hear that Daddy has not left yet, CCG make their own time. Good news about Ratzburg which is in Kreise Lauenberg and in our area. A nice old town situated on a lake right on the border with the Russian Zone. The cathedral is worth a visit, hardly damaged, and the Resident Officer is a Colonel Clark, pretty typical CCG, but on the few occasions our paths have crossed I have found him helpful. Pity you can't make Eutin I could have given you a personally conducted tour.

146 Relief Section, British Red Cross, BAOR 21 May 1947

The big news is that Renate and I have decided to get engaged. Last weekend I had a talk with Frau Schmalgemeyer, my German only just coped, but Renate came in at the end to help out. She was understanding and gave us her blessing, although as we expected she expressed some hesitations. She is very fond of Renate being the youngest and all that the family have been through. It will be hard for her to see her go, especially so far away. I think she quite likes me and has confidence in my ability to work to provide for us and so on. She expressed her concern about Elmar who she feels is a little restless and can be stubborn. Gisela and Elmar hope to marry in the summer, but as yet have nowhere to live. He is 24 and under apprenticeship with his father, but, of course the war set his progress back. Although it is common practice here we will not be having an engagement party or even announcing it publicly yet... Daddy phoned from Bad Oyenhausen yesterday morning, but we didn't

Clifford with British Red Cross Volkswagen, Spring 1947

have long to talk, so I couldn't tell him the news. He sounded cheerful, and said the journey over was calm and hopes to make Hannover for Whitsun, but is going to phone again later in the week...Rather busy at the moment as so many away... someone has just shouted that the water is hot so I must take the opportunity as I haven't had a bath for 10 days!

146 Relief Section, British Red Cross, BAOR 28 May 1947

Got back to Lübeck on Monday evening after a lovely Whitsun in Hannover. Daddy rang me again on Friday to say he was in Bad Nenndorf only a little west of Hannover. I couldn't get away on the Friday evening as I had hoped, as we had an official visitor from HQ to dinner. I left as early as possible on Saturday, but had to go via Rotenberg as I took two of our staff there for Whitsun. With Frank away I am acting as the Section Transport Officer so was able to take our Volkswagen car, the height of luxury, compared to our trucks. I got to the club where Daddy was staying at about 2 pm and then drove with him to Langenhagen and met everybody there. After much conversation and tea together we took some photos in the field behind the building Renate lives in. I had to take Daddy back soon after that as he was travelling to Berlin early the next day. Everyone liked him and was amazed at his fluent German. I am so glad the opportunity presented itself. Sunday was a bit of a come down, but we went for a drive in the car. I expect Daddy will tell you all when he gets home... Renate and I would like to take up yours and Freda's

Clifford and his father; Renate's mother and Clifford's father. Photographs taken in a field behind the Schmalgemeyer family's apartment.

offer to find an engagement ring for us, it is very kind and helpful of you both. It is virtually impossible to get anything here except on the black market and jewellery found there is not to be trusted. We would like a gold ring with a thin band and a single diamond stone, if that is not too expensive. I have little idea of prices, but something around £15 would fit my budget, with an absolute max of £30. One of the Red Cross women here has one which cost £70 and it doesn't look anything out of the ordinary. Will that be enough info. for you to go on? I hope you enjoy buying one and not having to pay! I am very grateful to you. I took the parcel with the jumpers for Renate with me, she was so thrilled. They were in such good condition and fitted her very well.

146 Relief Section, British Red Cross, BAOR 3 June 1947

By the time you get this Daddy should be home and told you all the news. He phoned me on the Friday before he left, but we couldn't arrange another meeting. I didn't finish work on Saturday till 2 pm and didn't get to Hannover till 7.30 pm, so another meeting here would not have been possible anyway. I had a short but pleasant weekend, but it was extraordinarily hot and difficult to sleep at night. The temperatures are supposed to be breaking records, and the 'white' population now take a siesta. Up here it is marvellous to be so near the seaside and we often take a dip in the sea in the evenings, the water is warm and it is hard to remember that only four months ago it was frozen over. I go to HQ at Vlotho on Monday much to my regret as I don't wish to leave Lübeck just now. I'll let you have the correct postal address when I get there, but please send any parcels here and they can wait my return. It's 11.30 pm and a bit cooler now so I think I will turn in, although it's still quite light and humid.

British Red Cross Commission, HQ 5, Civilian Relief, BAOR 11 June 1947

As you can see from the address I am now in Vlotho. I travelled to Hannover on Saturday and then came on here on Monday. The weather broke on Wednesday and it's been raining ever since. Despite the rain we had a good weekend and took some more snaps, but unfortunately the light got in and spoilt them, luckily we still have some film left. I may be here a little longer than I had anticipated as the person I'm filling in for doesn't leave until Friday, I had expected he would have already left by the time I arrived. Anyway I'm giving in my month's notice soon whatever happens. Frank Taylor in our Section got his release papers just before I left Lübeck, he is in group 50. I have to say I don't really find it very comfortable here, cooped up in an office with little to do, but maybe

Elmar Rössinger (Gisela's fiancé), Renate, Renate's mother, Gisela, Clifford

Vlotho on the river Weser. Note the destroyed road bridge over the river.

it will look up a bit when the person I take over from leaves. If not I shall be a little annoyed as I didn't want to come in the first place with the Section in Lübeck shorthanded. The atmosphere is a bit depressing, a sort of hotel kind of existence, with people coming and going, and most rather older than me so I tend to miss the comradeship, but it's early days, and I'm only here for three weeks anyway.

British Red Cross Commission, HQ5 Civilian Relief, BAOR 18 June 1947

Sorry if I sounded a bit depressed in my last letter, probably a combination of the mundane job and wet weather. Can't say there's been much improvement. I received a letter from the Civil Service to say that my application to enter the competitions had been turned down and my entrance fee refunded. I could be wrong but I have a feeling that my c.o. status did not help. I rated as a civilian although I had done alternative work overseas, and it was just as difficult to obtain information and send in forms as people in the forces. Service personnel are eligible even up to six months after the date of their release. Well it can't be helped it was only an idea anyway. I understand that only about 600 of the 4,000 applicants who pass the exams are accepted and two–thirds of these have to be ex-service personnel. Then on Friday night I chipped a bit off a front tooth biting on a toffee, the corner just cracked away. It isn't painful but it doesn't look very nice and spoils my smile! I suppose it will have to be crowned or something. I phoned the Army Dental Centre but they couldn't see me for three weeks and I shall be back in Lübeck by then. The Army dentist there may be able to fit me in, I went to him last

November, but if not it will have to wait until I get home... Sorry to hear Daddy had such a trying journey home... I went to Hannover for the weekend, it is only a short trip from here. Renate had some prints made from the photos we took recently, if we can find a shop with paper, there is a severe shortage, we will have copies made to send you.

William Hughes is based here but only looks in from time to time from his journeys round the Zone. He approached me and it would seem from his conversation that his wife had filled him in on my family background. I have to say I found him a bit vague. At breakfast the next day after we had been conversing for some minutes, he suddenly looked at me and said are you Clifford Barnard, just as though we had never spoken the day before. I must say he did look very tired and several times he said he was looking forward to returning to England as soon as a replacement could be found. *[For a brief account of his amazing work in Germany before and after the Second World War see the revised edition of* Sandbostel Revisited, *pp.182–87]* ... David Curtis looked in yesterday on his way home, he only got his release papers three days ago, Group 51. I've only got one more group to go! We agreed to meet in London with John on the 26th July, if as expected I get home on the 24th.

British Red Cross Commission, HQ5, Civilian Relief, BAOR 27 June 1947

Frank called in to HQ on his way home for good, so apart from Robin I am the last ex-FAU in the Section. He brought 15 items of post which had been waiting for me in Lübeck. Thank you for yours and the packets, especially the wool, which I will pass on to Renate, when I next go... As things stand at the moment I will leave Germany on 22 July. I am still allowed 7 days leave in Germany and 12 days in England with pay, before I have to sign off. I had arranged with some difficulty to book a few days with Renate in a guest house in Scharbeutz on the coast, but it has fallen through. They wrote to say they had been taken over by the local authorities and all the rooms requisitioned for refugees. It is too late to arrange anything else, but I can't complain as I know how great the need for refugee accommodation is. I may not have mentioned it before but someone else took over my responsibilities in Eutin before I went to Vlotho, but I shall be on call duty here next weekend so I shan't be going away. I drove over to Hannover the other evening to explain how things are. I shall probably go back to Lübeck on the 5th... I enclose a letter from Frau Andressen, who you may remember was the wife of the German PoW whom you invited to tea when I was home, and asked Daddy to send a parcel to his wife through me. It's rather a sweet letter...

British Red Cross Commission, HQ5, Civilian Relief, BAOR 2 July 1947

Time flies and I have so much to do before I leave for home. Thank you for all the letters especially the registered one with the ring in it! Thank you all for all the trouble you have gone to, I do appreciate it. I am sure Renate will like it. Thanks also for forwarding my release papers, I can hardly believe I'm a free man at last... I was most interested to hear of Daddy's conversation with Mr Jackson and the possibilities at H.K.Lewis *[medical and scientific publishers and booksellers]*, we will talk more about this when I get back... Jack Catchpool's scheme for bringing a group of young Germans to this country through the YHA in which it might be possible to include Renate sounds very promising. I'll get Renate to give me all the necessary particulars and if possible I will try and visit Herr Schlichter, head of the Jugendherberger in Hannover, who you may remember Martin Southwood and I worked with for a short time about a year ago. With contacts at both ends it might help to make it more possible...

146 Relief Section, British Red Cross, BAOR 9 July 1947

I got back here on Tuesday after doing a small job in Hamburg on the way up. Now I have to tackle all the packing up. The Section is holding a party on Saturday evening, when many of the people I have had contact with while I have been here will be invited. I hope to be able to fetch Renate as well. At present my timetable is that I shall have four days in Hannover next week, return to Lübeck and then finally leave here on Tuesday 22nd, staying for a day in Vlotho before catching the train the next day, so I should be home sometime on the 24th... I managed to get to Renate's to give her the ring, she was very excited, thought it was lovely and it could hardly have fitted better. All the family had to examine it and Annelotte and Gisela compared it with their rings, but I will tell you more soon. As I feared the large parcel had been pilfered and the raincoat was missing, very disappointing. The wool seemed to be all there, but not knowing exactly what was in it I can't say for sure if anything else was taken... The Section is going to be very depleted. Frank and two others have gone, I and another this month, leaving only three people. The work has been slowly reduced so I imagine there will not be any replacements and will, I suppose, be closed fairly soon... I'm glad to have left HQ, it was an interesting experience to have had, but I didn't find it very congenial.

As from 146 Relief Section, British Red Cross, BAOR 16 July 1947

This is almost certainly my last letter from Germany. I'm experiencing very mixed emotions – miserable about not knowing how long I shall be parted from Renate, 'demob happy' but having strange feelings about leaving the places where I have had so many experiences in last two years, and not knowing what is before me. I am staying at Renate's for four days but will return to Lübeck on Sunday. Then to Vlotho to hand in bits of kit and so on, and next day homeward bound. I have a number of papers concerning the termination of my contract with BRC, almost as complicated to leave as to join! When I arrive in London I have to go to the Red Cross offices in Grosvenor Square and see Lady Falmouth, who has recently taken over from Lady Mountbatten. Then I have to be medically examined, x-rayed and so on, and finally clear up with the Finance and Equipment departments. I will still be due for 12 days paid leave.

Before I came here to Renate's I tied up my work and packed all my belongings, sending three parcels home to you, but please don't bother to open them, they can wait until I get there. I had to buy another grip bag to take things with me that I shall need... The party was good fun, I did manage to fetch Renate, and there were some twenty-five people who came – British, German, Danish, Estonian, Canadian and a South African. We didn't finish till the early hours and then I still had to take Geoffrey Levy's brother, who is a doctor in the RAF, back to his station not too far away. *[Geoffrey Levy was at school with me, but I can't recall how his brother got involved!]* On the way back dawn was breaking, but I managed some kip before getting up at 8 am, grabbed some breakfast and set off for Hannover soon after 9 am. At the Hauptbahnhof in Hannover I left an English girl, a friend of Robin's, who was at the party, she works for the CCG and was catching a train for Brussels. On the Monday I returned the vehicle to Lübeck as it will be needed there, and on Tuesday I hitch hiked to Hamburg and caught a military train to Hannover and then tram and bus to Langenhagen. Quite a bit of travelling. I'm writing this while Renate is in college, she doesn't start her holiday until tomorrow. I got a nice surprise – just as the party was about to start, who should turn up but Reg Middleton. I haven't seen or heard from him for a very long time. He has been working for IGCR *[Intergovernmental Committee for Refugees]* mainly in the American Zone but they packed up in June so found himself a temporary job, but as he had a pocketful of American dollars he thought he would have a couple of weeks in Denmark before returning home. Although he appeared very carefree I thought there was an underlying sadness and it turned out that Celia [Newton] and he had broken off their engagement at Easter. He was released about five months ago but took up further work rather than return home, and is now considering emigrating. Although he has a sister in the USA, he thought he would try New Zealand first. It was nice to catch up with him though, he is such a pleasant easy going fellow. He thought I had changed a lot but he didn't say in what way!

Epilogue

I returned to England for good on 25 July 1947, exactly four years after leaving school in July 1943 to fulfil the conditions laid down by my conscientious objectors tribunal. In August I went on a two week holiday with my parents to the Lake District, staying in a guest house at Boot in Eskdale. Among other hills, my father and I climbed Scafell via Cam Spout, for the first time.

Towards the end of 1947 Renate came to England on a short visit under an Anglo-German youth project organised by Jack Catchpool through the YHA. Christmas was spent with my parents, who had again invited two German soldiers, from a nearby PoW camp, who originated from Hannover and Lübeck, to share Christmas dinner. Renate and I were able to bring them news of their home towns. It was wonderful to see Renate again and for her to get some idea of where she would be living after we were married.

Renate and I were married on 10 July 1948 at the Friends Meeting House in Welwyn Garden City and had our honeymoon in Aldeburgh, Suffolk, staying in a cabin in the grounds of my Aunt Connie's house. We had three children, Mark, Anthony and Jennifer.

In September 1947 I had started work at H.K. Lewis & Co. Ltd., medical and scientific publishers and booksellers, in Gower Street, London. First I was researching the information to reply to letters enquiring about books on all aspects of medicine, from doctors, scientists, hospitals, universities, institutions and libraries from around the world. Later I was put in charge of a new department, Research and Publicity, which was created around my work. In addition to the considerable correspondence, records were kept of customers' interests, so that they could be advised on new literature as it became available. Regular subject catalogues and monthly and

8   THE WELWYN TIMES

GERMAN BRIDE

First German bride in WGC since the war was Fraulein Renate Schmalgemeyer, physical training instructress, of Hanover. The bridegroom was Mr Clifford Barnard, of 78 Woodhall Lane, WGC. The couple met when Mr Barnard was working with the Friends Ambulance Unit in Germany in 1946. They were married at the Friends Meeting House.

weekly lists were prepared and distributed. With its vast lending library H.K.Lewis was a unique institution and it was little short of academic vandalism when in the 1980s it was sold to a competitor who then promptly closed it down.

Before this occurred I had left the firm in 1965 when I was appointed Assistant General Secretary of the Friends Home Service Committee of the Religious Society of Friends at Friends House in London, later renamed

Quaker Home Service and now known as Quaker Life. The department's responsibilities have changed over the years, but it has been essentially concerned with sustaining the fabric of Quaker life, deepening the spiritual life of Friends and Meetings, and promoting outreach both locally and nationally. The department has offered opportunities for support and learning for those with special responsibilities in local Meetings, such as elders, overseers, clerks, wardens and others. It has helped develop local and regional networks for pastoral care and the handling of queries and crises.

Increasingly my main occupation became Quaker literature for Friends and those wishing to learn more about Quaker beliefs and attitudes, which was selected, commissioned, published and distributed through the Quaker Bookshop. Much of this work was carried out through a number of functional committees, which I helped to service, often as secretary.

Sandbostel Revisited

Revised 2009 from the pamphlet of 2001

1. Introduction

The publication of *Two Weeks in May 1945* in October 1999 received far more notice than I had anticipated without the promotional facilities of a commercial publisher. There were a number of reviews, not only in the Quaker press as one might expect, but also in other religious papers, notably a double column in the *Church Times*. My local newspaper the *Welwyn Times* gave the book half a page, while a new national monthly *Men's Quest* included a six page article on conscientious objection, following an interview with myself, with several photographs from the book. I talked live with John Pilgrim in his 'Out and About' programme on BBC Three Counties Radio in their Luton studios. In May 2000, around the 55th anniversary of the liberation of Sandbostel Camp, a documentary based on the book was shown on Radio Bremen TV and later on Radio Hamburg TV, which included interviews with Elfie Walther who as a very young woman had been one of those brought in to help, Dr Hans Engel, a British Army doctor who cared for the inmates, and myself.

It was most heart-warming to receive appreciative letters over the ensuing months. One or two were from people who had been at Sandbostel, either as inmates, rescuers, or helpers. I realised that their often moving stories would have added so much to the book, had I known of them when I was doing the research, and I felt I would like to make this new material available in the form of a follow-up booklet. *Sandbostel Revisited* was issued privately in 2001 with only a small print run and was soon unavailable, so when the decision was made to publish my letters home in book form it seemed an opportunity to include a revised edition of the booklet. I hope that those who read *Two Weeks in May 1945* but did not see *Sandbostel Revisited* will appreciate this revised edition and find these further experiences of equal interest.

Several of the writers of the letters to me, although admiring Quaker principles, expressed the belief that at times force was necessary to overcome something as evil as Hitler. It seemed right, therefore, to include a chapter trying to explain in a very personal way how I now see these things in the light of events since 1945.

I would like to gratefully acknowledge the permission of all those who wrote to me following the publication of the book to quote, sometimes extensively, from their letters. In particular, Gwendoline Versteeg, Dr Hans Engel, Dr Gwenda Barer and Hugo Zaugg, and Elfie Walther for the extensive extracts from her diary; also Hans König who in 1947 painted the water colour of the camp (p.186), while a detainee of the British Army in the Civilian Internment Camp at Sandbostel. After so many years it has not been possible to trace him, so I hope he will forgive me for using it without his permission. The story of how this painting came into my possession is told on page 187. Please note that the *TWIM* page numbers refer to the pages in *Two Weeks in May 1945* where the subject is first mentioned.

2. A *Survivor*

Probably the most unexpected but very welcome letter was from Gwendoline Versteeg, the wife of a Dutch survivor of the Camp – Adrianus Jacobus Hendrikus Versteeg, now living in the USA. She had been sent a copy of *Two Weeks in May 1945* by a friend, and on reading my remark that 'My main regret is that after all these years I have not been able to trace any of the ex-inmates' (*TWIM* p.111), she felt compelled to write to me with his remarkable story:

> You see, my husband was a member of the Dutch Resistance and was imprisoned as a political prisoner at Sandbostel. He was among the human skeletons that crawled in the filth and miraculously liberated on April 29th, 1945. Yes, we believe in miracles! He had been transported in a closed cattle truck from Meppen-Versen (6 days) to Farge and after nine days transported again in a cattle truck destined for Bergen-Belsen and the gas chambers. The train reached Celle and was then directed back as Bergen-Belsen had been liberated the day before – this journey lasted eleven days, five of them without a scrap of food. The final destination was Sandbostel. He had been operated on his foot to remove gangrene at Meppen-Versen and was unable to walk.

> Adrian has little memory of the first days of freedom. He does remember the delicious taste of sugar water on his shrivelled tongue and of the shadowy figures (soldiers) standing in the door-

way, speaking English, and offering him an American cigarette. He does know he was in a British Field Hospital at Rotenburg as he has the Field Medical Card recording the transfusions and injections. It also shows he was a patient in Block E Room 36, bed 9. An English doctor, Captain Blumfield, examined him and German nurses tended to his care. Gradually he became aware and in his letters home (yes, we have these too) he mentions looking at the pine trees through the window.

In June he was moved by the Dutch Red Cross to a monastery in Harreveld that had been converted into a field hospital. He was worried by all the dying that seemed endless and longing to go home and at his own risk he was allowed to go to an uncle in Oldenzaal on 27th June and finally returned to The Hague on the 25th of July. He was then 23 years old. His family – parents and two brothers – had endured the 'hunger winter' but sadly his father died in December. Adrian was invited with other Resistance friends to go to Denmark for recuperation.

Although active in the Dutch Resistance Adrian Versteeg's weapon had not been a gun but a pen. Gwendoline explains:

He forged and falsified German documents. He worked with German doctors at an Employment Bureau in The Hague where fellow Dutchmen were medically examined *en route* to labour camps in Germany. All, or most, were reluctant to leave their homes so he learned the codes and falsified the results. Hundreds were saved in this way. Adrian also forged the signatures of the German officials on stolen identity cards and distributed ration cards and money to people in hiding. In 1982 Prince Bernhard presented him with the Resistance Cross in Washington DC with others who had also emigrated to the USA. One of the German doctors, Dr Hugo Kirchgaesser, befriended Adrian, and as Adrian was fluent in German, as well as English and French so he was able to converse with the older man and later correspond. But after the war, his letters offering help were returned. Adrian always felt he was not a Nazi.

Gwendoline goes on to describe how she first met Adrian in San Remo, Italy and again later in London in 1953 during the coronation celebrations, when they confirmed their feelings for each other. However, Adrian had decided to leave Holland and start a new life in America without the constant reminders of the war. But for Gwendoline leaving home presented a dilemma. As with many thousands of other children she had been evacuated from London in 1939 at the age of eleven and had been away from home for three and a half years, and had no desire to go to America and leave her loved ones again. But Adrian could not abandon his wish for her to join him and returned to England a year later to persuade her to share his life, and they finally married in the USA in 1956. Gwendoline went on to write that

> Adrian never talked about his days in the concentration camps, but as the years sped by he felt a great need to be able to thank the people who had given him back his life. We had assumed the English speaking soldiers were American because of the Chesterfield cigarettes and so were never able to get any definite leads. Then my brother in Brighton read a book that clearly stated it was the British Army who had liberated the Camp. In 1995, when we planned to be in Europe for the commemorations of VE Day a friend of mine placed a notice in *Saga*, a magazine for senior citizens, asking if anyone had been at the liberation of Sandbostel, as an ex-inmate wished to personally thank his liberators for his life.

When they arrived in England 14 replies were waiting for them. One was from Frank Westby of Lancaster and another from Dennis Turnbull of Morpeth, who invited Adrian to attend the final reunion of the 4th Durham Survey Regiment. They stayed two nights with Dennis and his wife Kathleen, who Gwendoline said were wonderful hosts. Gwendoline and Adrian had flown to Newcastle from Amsterdam and Adrian was finally able to thank those who had been at Sandbostel. 'It had long been our desire to let these soldiers (all young boys at the time) know that somebody had survived this horror camp and had been able to live a wonderful life. The report of the gathering stated that Adrian's visit had been the icing on the cake! In Amsterdam we attended a memorial service and laid flowers at the monument'.

On their return to America, a reporter for the *Salt Lake Tribune*, who had previously been in contact with them for an article on the Dutch in the city, approached them seeking to write an article on the meeting with his liberators. The article developed into writing Adrian's memoirs, firstly for his family, but the reporter later sought permission to publish it as a book*. Gwendoline wrote that the book tells all of Adrian's life and how in later years he came to see that it was the Nazis not the Germans who were responsible for his suffering. She wrote in her letter:

*Tony Semerad, 'A Life Saved'. I have been unable to trace whether this was ever published; it is not in the British Library or Library of Congress catalogues.

Adrian was the President of the Dutch soccer club in Salt Lake City and he changed it into a international social club. Dances were held every month with a band led by a German accordion player. Many of the members were German and became our friends – all various nationalities blended together for a happy time. Adrian was President for 25 years.

In 1969 Adrian suffered a severe heart attack and since then has been a heart patient with all its associated limitations. He had diphtheria twice in the camps and Gwendoline believes that this no doubt caused some weakness to his heart. She concluded her letter to me by saying:

> …it is meant as a tribute to you for the courage and compassion you gave to so many like Adrian, when you were so young. 'A Life Saved' conveys Adrian's desire to make his life worthwhile in a very special way. Our family would not be if you and others like you had not given of yourselves – one day later would have been too late for Adrian. Each day is precious to us.

This last comment is particularly poignant as Gwendoline has herself had cancer twice and a brain tumour. Then in April 2005, six years after *Two Weeks in May 1945* was published, I received a final card, which read,

> On April 29th we will celebrate 60 years of Adrian's liberation from Sandbostel. Adrian is now 83 and although he does not have robust health he enjoys every day. It is quite remarkable that the lice covered skeleton, crawling through the filth, awaiting death, was saved and given his life. It must be satisfying to you all – so brave and experiencing such frightening situations that it culminated in such a perfect and exceptional gift. Celebrate with us the part you played in making such a miracle.

> Our love and God bless you – Gwen and Adrian Versteeg.

3. Another Rescuer and Some Reactions

In *Two Weeks in May 1945* (pp.20–24 and 108–110), I described some of the experiences of Captain Robert Barer, an RAMC doctor, when he was the first officer to enter the concentration camp, so it was of great interest, after its publication, to receive a letter from another RAMC doctor, Dr Hans Engel.

He was born in Hamburg of Jewish parents during the First World War. In 1935, at the age of 19, after completing his *Abitur* (school leaving and university entrance exam) he was allowed as a 'non-Aryan' to emigrate to Britain where he studied medicine in Edinburgh. Following nine months internment in the Isle of Man and Canada, as an enemy alien, he returned to take his medical exams in 1941. After working in hospitals in Manchester and Rotherham and later in general practice in White-haven, he joined the British Army as a medical officer. He took part in the D-Day Normandy invasion on June 6th, 1944, and then in the campaign through France, Belgium, Holland and Germany, as a Regimental Medical Officer, first as a Captain, but later promoted to Major. He was taken personally to Sandbostel by the Director of Medical Services of 30 Corps, as he was known to speak fluent German.

In his letter Dr Engel described how he entered Sandbostel Camp, on his 29th birthday, the day after its liberation, with 'three other RAMC officers and some thirty other ranks and also a Hygiene Section', who were responsible for the DDT delousing of personal and patients (these men were almost certainly from the 168 Light Field Ambulance and 31 Field Hygiene Section; see *TWIM* p.27). They all had to work in the ter-rible dirt and stench of the huts for three weeks. Dr Engel explained:

> Most victims had to be treated with intravenous fluids, and we were fortunate to obtain some anaesthetists, who were expert at getting into collapsed veins, to give glucose and plasma till the patients were able to retain fluids taken orally. I had two men on a large cauldron making warm drinks all day from the contents of PoW Red Cross parcels released to us as they were no longer needed *[the prisoners of war were in the process of being sent home]*. So we had plenty of Ovaltine, Horlicks and chocolate drinks, which doubtless saved many lives. Once the patients were rehydrated and no longer vomiting they were washed and deloused *[this would have been the 'human laundry' described in TWIM pp.34–35]* and taken to the 'hospital' huts...

With his letter to me Dr Engel enclosed copies of three letters that he had written at the time to his uncle and aunt, Otto and Margaret, who had more or less been his family *in loco parentis* in England. The original letters are now deposited in the Department of Documents at the Imperial War Museum in London. In one of these letters dated 11 June 1945 he wrote:

> As you know, I spent three weeks in Sandbostel Camp dealing with Typhus. I think I must have dealt with several hundreds myself, and I was running a ward for the worst cases, it was a very busy and at times very uphill job. It was all a matter of feeding and sanitation, of course we could do no real nursing, everybody was busy with making food and diets and trying to improve 'living' conditions. It was an immense task, but we reduced the mortality

from 120 to one a day by the end. Of course all you could do would not save hundreds, and they had to die before you saw results. When you consider the thousands that died before we got there, it was just a drop in the bucket, and most of the worst cases were better dead anyway. Still it was amazing to see people, who had been systematically made into animals, become human again and often regain sanity and decency, and even manners in a very short time. It was an awful job, made more difficult with the mixture of nationalities – a very tower of Babel! I shall always remember our Major trying to give directions to a Russian doctor. I stood next to him and translated into German, a Polish doctor on my other side then translated into Russian, and after animated discussion the Russian's answers came back the whole row, this going backwards and forwards all the time... I spent VE day and night amongst dying, starved or typhus and TB ridden humanity – if such it can be called – I wonder how many will ever be human again.

In *Two Weeks in May 1945* I wrote, 'The tasks the German women and nurses had to undertake were highly dangerous, because of widespread typhus, but they were so horrified by what they saw they worked willingly' (*TWIM* p.71). Dr Engel commented that his experience had been a little different. He wrote to me in his letter:

Regarding the women who were brought in to work there I vividly remember that we collected nurses by three-ton trucks from Hamburg, Eppendorf, Barmbeck and Bremen hospitals. When they arrived in a very truculent mood their matron said to me, 'We are not going to risk our health for half-men (*Halbmenschen*)'. Thereupon I gave them the lecture of my life (and theirs), to point out that the British Army men were working there day and night trying to save lives a lot more valuable than theirs and that the British had much less responsibility for their state than the Germans, who knew quite well what was going on in the KZs *[concentration camps]*. After that they really worked hard even on the worst cases. Three weeks later the matron asked to speak with me. She said she had never been so ashamed to be German as on the day I had lectured them all. So it was hardly correct to state that these women worked there willingly, at least from the beginning.

The nurses Dr Engel refers to would have been a little older than the high school girls from Delmenhorst who had travelled with the Mil. Gov./ FAU convoy. Because of the pressure of work and the language difficulties, we FAU had little communication with these young women, apart from immediate matters to do with the jobs in hand, so we learnt little of their feelings. I could only write the book from my own experience, but accept that it was necessarily limited. However, I feel that my words, based on both my own and my colleagues' observations on the return of the women to Delmenhorst after two weeks, are still valid: 'They were still shocked at what they had experienced, some were sick, all worn out, and did not wish to communicate, but they had all worked without restraint to the point of exhaustion' (*TWIM* page 85).

When undertaking the research before writing *Two Weeks in May 1945* I invited, through a notice in a local German newspaper, anybody who had worked in Sandbostel at the time to write to me with their experiences. All who replied expressed their horror and shame that German people could have committed these atrocities, and were adamant that these things should never be allowed to happen again anywhere in the world (*TWIM* pages 71-85). Further to Dr Engel's remarks I can only say that as far as the many women drafted in from the surrounding villages were concerned, they appeared genuinely horrified at what they found, and said they had only known Sandbostel as a camp for prisoners of war. In this connection Captain Barer's remarks are of interest. Although born in England he was the son of Russian Jews who had emigrated to England in 1914. He was very concerned that all Germans should be made aware of what had happened. He left Sandbostel after ten days and found himself in charge of the German Naval and Military hospitals in the Cuxhaven area and promptly arranged for a group of German doctors on the staff and a lawyer to visit Sandbostel. After they had spoken to the German doctors and nurses still working at the Camp, he observed their profound and genuine shock, and wrote in his report,

I hold no brief for the German people but it is only fair to say that my considered opinion is that the vast majority of them knew nothing of the conditions inside the concentration camps. These places were closely guarded by the SS and no ordinary German was allowed anywhere near them. Those few who were released after serving a term were far too terrified of returning to relate any experiences... (Robert Barer, *One Young Man and Total War*, 1998, p.286)

In *Two Weeks in May 1945* I reflected on my own experiences:

Although in the immediate situation I had little time to think deeply of these things, I did experience an overpowering feeling of the enormity of the horror I was confronting and I wondered how such things could come about. I believe we all have the capacity for evil, none of us knows how we would have behaved under Nazi rule. But I know also that each of us has the capacity for good, the ability to recognise the human being in the stranger. How was it then that every day somebody had stood in those wooden towers looking down on people dying and crying out for help? How was it that people had fired guns at those starving people trying to raid the kitchen for food? (*TWIM* p.107)

Again Captain Barer's remarks are of interest. In his 'Report on Sandbostel' referred to earlier, he described how he first entered the Camp accompanied by a Captain Wilcox, a former Adjutant and now a press representative, and his English-speaking German medical orderly, Otto. His descriptions of the appalling and horrific conditions they found take two or three pages. As they walked back through the trees to give their report to the Army units waiting to enter the Camp and start the rescue operation he realised something for the first time:

'Did you feel any pity?' I asked Captain Wilcox. 'No', he replied. 'It's a strange thing isn't it?' It was true. The things we had seen were so terrible that all feelings of sympathy or pity had been driven out. All I felt was horror, disgust, and I am ashamed to admit it hate. Hate against the prisoners for looking as they did, for living as they did, for existing at all. It was quite unreasonable but there it was, and it gave us one possible explanation of why the SS had done those things. Once having reduced their prisoners to such a state the only emotions the guards could feel were loathing, disgust and hate. Do not think I am apologising for the SS, I am not... but I am merely trying to find some reason for their extraordinary behaviour. (Robert Barer, p.283)

Similarly, William Hitchcock tells in his book *Liberation* how many Allied soldiers were disgusted and repulsed by the 'ape-like gibbering skeletons' they liberated from the death camps, and so could not relate to them as fellow human beings.

I do believe we are all responsible for our actions, but recognise that there are evil situations in which we can all find ourselves, where our civilised part can be lost. When suffering happens, we often want to look away.

4. Some Other Stories

In *Two Weeks in May 1945* (pp.28–29) I described how a party of about 60 high school girls from Delmenhorst were among the many people drafted in to help clear up the Camp, and travelled with the Mil. Gov / FAU convoy. Elfie Walther was one of this group. Although she did not respond to my notice in the *Weser-Kurier*, I heard of her from Gwenda Barer, the widow of Captain Barer. Elfie Walther had kept a diary during her time at Sandbostel and extracts from it were included by Robert Barer in *One Young Man and Total War*, and by Ulrike Jordan in *Conditions of Surrender: British and Germans Witness the End of the War* (London: Tauris Academic Studies, 1997). The documentary film on Sandbostel shown on German TV in May 2000 around the 55th anniversary of the Camp's liberation (see p.171), included an interview with her. This diary gives a penetrating insight into what this vulnerable girl was experiencing.

On April 28 an English officer and a German policeman brought her a letter to report to the Town Hall 'with things for several days'. Her mother feared she would be sent away as a foreign worker, but Elfie recorded on May 1:

> We have been told that we are to clear up a camp near Hamburg. I got a dreadful shock ...a concentration camp! I had heard enough about them over the last few days. I hope we don't have to go into the camp with all those dead people, I thought...

She continues, later that evening:

> I have just heard the most terrible news. I must write it down today. We have one candle, so it's possible... In the hospital barrack were three old medical orderlies from the time when the camp housed PoWs. They told us things that gave us shivers down the spine.

and the next day she writes of how she 'couldn't stop thinking about how we had loved and honoured the Fuehrer', and her disillusionment:

> Last night I finished with everything that I used to believe was good. People are vile pigs – all of them, including me. And there is meant to be a God? And he allows all this to happen? ... I haven't seen a prisoner yet, and I notice that I am glad. I am frightened of seeing them. How can we apologise?

> May 4, evening. It is cruel in the typhus barracks. I lack the right words to describe all the misery. They are hardly people. Skeletons lie there in their filthy beds, smeared with excrement from head to foot, and stare at us with huge eyes... How ashamed I am in these minute to be German! We caused this!

> May 6, 1945. More and more sick people are being brought in. There are six barracks in our complex, and all are overcrowded.

Another 600 new patients are to be brought today. But yesterday and today more than 100 people died… Our mental state is much worse than our physical condition. We will never lose these impressions…

By the evening of May 6, a number of her companions have dropped out and she has to do the work in one barracks alone. Some of the patients have become quite aggressive, but

Thank goodness there is one room with nice, educated people in it. They come from Holland and Belgium. Some of them are doctors, and a lawyer, who always consoles and encourages us. Just imagine: someone who has suffered so much at the hands of our people encourages us!

May 7, 1945. The suffering here is so dreadful. Sometimes I think I can no longer bear it. So many people die. Wrapped in blankets, these skeletons walk – or rather stagger – between the barracks. There really are children – gypsy children – among them. I can't understand it! They even put children in concentration camps…

On May 10 her group are suddenly told they will be leaving the next day, and 100 girls from Bremen arrive to replace them – 'They didn't even have any luggage with them – and thought they were just going to look at the camp. Well, they'll have a good look round!' On her return, she realises:

While we were away, nobody knew where we were… It is nice to be home, but it is different from how it was before. I have experienced too many dreadful things. One needs time to cope with it… I haven't told anybody anything, although everybody asks all the time. I simply can't yet. Perhaps I am afraid that they won't believe me?

She notes in a postscript that at least 25 of her friends went down with typhus, and after her return everyone in her house had lice.

My parents were speechless when one evening, I told them about the horrors. A world collapsed for them too, and at that time we didn't even know everything I had seen was nothing compared with what had happened in other camps, especially the extermination camps.

Another interesting letter I received was from Ted Kelk. As a soldier, also in the 4th Durham Survey Regiment, he was posted to Sandbostel on the 6th May 1945 for guard duties. Three days later he fell ill and it was thought he might have contracted typhus, but fortunately this proved not to be the case. He was cared for by 3 Field Dressing Station until the 12th May, when he returned to his unit in Sandbostel village, and on the 28th May was moved to Cuxhaven. A close friend, Michael Carey, with whom he remained in touch all his life, wrote a long letter to his fiancé while at Sandbostel, recounting in considerable detail the camp and all the degradation and horrors that were found there. This letter, now deposited in the Department of Documents at the Imperial War Museum, confirmed much of what I had read during my research and what I had personally experienced. Ted Kelk was deeply affected by his experience of war and, following the dropping of the atomic bombs on Hiroshima and Nagasaki which he felt must mean either the end of mankind or the end of war, he turned to pacifism. During the 1950s he and his wife joined the Religious Society of Friends, as he did not wish to be a pacifist in isolation.

Although I did not hear again from any of the other women who had kindly responded to my original request in the *Weser-Kurier* in May 1997 (*TWIM*, p.72), I was touched to receive a birthday card from Gertraude Walsdorf in February 2000. During a rather chaotic time during the fighting in the Rhineland I had written in a letter home which I quoted in *Two Weeks in May 1945*, 'On the 25th of February I realised some days later that my twentieth birthday on the 18th had passed unnoticed...'(*TWIM*, p.12). In the card, which included a beautiful poem, Gertraude had written, 'Reading your book I came across your birthday and wanted to let you know 55 years later it is not forgotten on the continent this year! I wish you many happy returns and all health and happiness.' She went on to thank me for writing the book and described how during a difficult time in Schleswig-Holstein with her family she had received British help, and how a Welsh lady living in Kent became her dearest friend. 'How grateful we should be for peaceful lives. God bless you', she ended.

5. Another Quaker Connection

An unexpected further Quaker connection with Sandbostel was revealed in a letter from a Swiss Friend, Hugo Zaugg. As a young man he had joined the Friends Relief Service and was posted as a driver and interpreter to William R. Hughes, a British Friend whose extraordinary work in Germany both before and after the war deserves an entire book devoted to it. I knew him slightly as he attended Welwyn Garden City Quaker Meeting and was acquainted with my parents.

In Germany before the war he had worked together with another remarkable Quaker, Corder Catchpool, on behalf of the victims of Nazi persecution. He greatly admired Corder and later told his story in a book, *Indomitable Friend* (Allen & Unwin, 1956). Roger Wilson writing in *Quaker Relief* (Allen & Unwin, 1952) records that William Hughes, '... made himself so unpopular with the Nazi authorities for his fearless befriending of their victims that they threw him out of Germany and forbade his return...' (p.259). During the war, his concern for prisoners led him to make his home on the Isle of Man so that he could be of service to those civilian aliens who had been interned there by the British authorities. He also visited widely throughout Britain in camps set up for German prisoners of war. Further references to William Hughes and Corder Catchpool are given in Hans A. Schmitt, *Quakers and Nazis: Inner light in outer darkness* (University of Missouri Press, 1997).

In the Spring of 1945, following the cessation of hostilities, many voluntary societies, including the Friends Relief Service, sent Relief teams into Germany under the auspices of the Council of British Societies for Relief Abroad (COBSRA) and the British Red Cross, to join others like the FAU teams already working there with Displaced Persons and concentration camp victims. In the autumn of that year the increasingly desperate needs of the German civilians became more apparent and many of the teams transferred their concern to this area of work. Earlier in this volume, on p.142, I make reference to an informative article that appeared in *The Guardian* in 1946 by Richard Law MP, who as chairman of COBSRA outlined some of the work being carried out by these teams.

The British Army established six Civilian Internment Camps (CIC) and a War Criminal Holding Centre at Fischberg, near Hamburg. One of these camps was located at Sandbostel and another at Neuengamme, using some of the remaining buildings on the sites of the former concentration camps. I made a passing reference to this in *Two Weeks in May 1945* (p.114), 'Until 1948 some SS and other National Socialist functionaries were imprisoned there'. The Friends Relief Service made it a special concern to visit amongst the people interned in these camps and help in anyway they could. This work suited William Hughes very well and he started his visiting '...in September 1946, intending to spend six months on it, but found such need that he stayed on until November 1947, when he was reluctantly compelled to return to England, and another Friend, William Lyon, was found to replace him' (Roger Wilson, *Quaker Relief*, p.259). In my letter home dated 18 June 1947 (p. 165) I mention a meeting with William Hughes while at the British Red Cross HQ at Vlotho and wrote, 'I must say he did look very tired and several times he said he was looking forward to returning to England as soon as a replacement could be found'.

The work William Hughes undertook was unusual and Roger Wilson explained in *Quaker Relief* (p.259) that

There were two main categories among the internees. Some were awaiting trial, charged with some known atrocity, or war crime; they were segregated. The remainder, and by far the larger number, with whom the Quaker workers were more generally concerned, were interned simply on grounds of potential danger to the community – men who had held positions in the Nazi Party or belonged to one of the organisations condemned at Nuremberg *[the trial of 22 Nazi leaders conducted by an international military tribunal from November 1945 to October 1946]*. The cases of these men were heard individually by the appropriate German or British security tribunals, but this screening was a desperately slow business... William Hughes described the internees: 'In this mixture are of course many black sheep (mostly known by now) but a far larger number of decent citizens and soldiers, once followers of Hitler, now pretty thoroughly disillusioned, no worse than the average citizens outside'.

In December 1945 there were some 50,000 internees contained in these seven camps. Although conditions behind the wire were rigorous and dreary they were not physically brutal, but communication with the outside world was very limited. The prolonged isolation, anxiety as to how their families were faring in the deprived post-war conditions, the lack of occupation and sense of injustice with regard to their detention, had resulted in a very low morale. William Hughes and Hugo Zaugg moved about the British Zone, spending a week or so in the neighbourhood of each camp in turn and visiting daily.

After introducing themselves to the British officer in charge of the camp and discussing with him problems that arose there, they would go on to strike up acquaintance with internees who took a leading part in camp life. The men, who came predominately from the educated classes, had usually developed an elaborate system of activities within the camps – schools, churches, theatres, sports, handicrafts, choirs, orchestras – in an effort to resist mental stagnation, and it was not difficult to find instances where outsiders' help with small supplies of materials and tools could be of real value...There was an insatiable demand for reading material on all subjects, in all languages, and an appeal to Friends and others in Britain brought in a most welcome supply of books and periodicals (Roger Wilson, p.259).

William Hughes and Hugo Zaugg found an eagerness among the prisoners to communicate with anyone from the outside world and they had many opportunities to talk in both groups and private conversation,

Naturally we hear a good deal of their hardships and grievances. But mostly we discuss all the many problems facing Germany and the world, problems of race, education, social organization, religion, international relations, and so on. With the failure of their Nazi beliefs, some of the men had developed a hard cynicism reinforced by the knowledge that while they were interned for supposed misdemeanours, others of their colleagues with perhaps less honesty, walked about free outside. Others were seeking with intense and serious need for new valid ideas to replace the broken ones (Roger Wilson, p.259).

In May 1947, he was invited to speak to the men in the camps over Hamburg Radio in a broadcast in which he summed up in words the spiritual sense of what he and his colleagues were trying to express by their work in the camps.

Quakers in Britain were troubled by the prolongation of the indiscriminate internment, '...and early in 1947 William Hughes sought an interview with the Lord Chancellor and Lord Pakenham in which he urged measures to obviate the men's long wait for judicial hearing' (Roger Wilson, p.259). It is not possible to know what weight the interviews had, but during the summer the camps were rearranged according to a new policy and the process of bringing the internees before their boards was accelerated. In January 1948 it was announced that all camps would be cleared, excepting the one holding war-crime suspects.

In his letter to me Hugo Zaugg told me how he and William Hughes had free access to the internees and were never searched but they had agreed to the strict regulation not to convey letters. The British Commandant of Sandbostel, a Colonel Vickers, was highly regarded by the German inmates. He supported their cultural activities to avoid idleness and boredom, and granted leave of absence on parole in cases of emergency. Gardening competitions were arranged in a rather unpromising countryside. A group was formed for those interested in painting and drawing who were allowed out of camp, to pursue these activities. Hugo Zaugg commented that it was refreshing to see these out of camp paintings, without images of the barbed wire which must have been ever present in their minds. A group of women from a theatre company in Hamburg were invited to participate in camp productions, as Colonel Vickers did not want the men to play women's parts. There could hardly have been a greater contrast to the regime run by the Nazis at Sandbostel in earlier years.

Hugo Zaugg related how every two months or so William Hughes would report to Brigadier Ingham, Head of the Legal Branch of the British Control Commission in Germany at Herford, on their experiences

Hans König's watercolour of Sandbostel Camp in 1947

with the internees. On several occasions he expressed his view that the CIC at Sandbostel despite its difficult situation was being run on a very humane basis. On one occasion Brigadier Ingham remarked that William Hughes seemed to be very well informed on English legal procedures, to which he replied that he had formerly been a barrister. Hugo Zaugg recalled another instance when they delivered a supply of books, paper, pencils and other materials for the use of study groups at the war Criminal Holding Centre at Fischbeck. They discovered that the Welfare Officer, a Major Ball, and William Hughes were old acquaintances. Before the war in Welwyn Garden City he had arranged children's parties where William Hughes had led ornithological excursions.

Hugo Zaugg sent me a water colour painted by an inmate, Hans König, showing a part of Sandbostel Camp in 1947 while it was under British administration. The painting was used in colour as the front cover for the first, separately published edition of *Sandbostel Revisited*. The fence of barbed wire and the watch towers are the same as in May 1945, but the flowers in the tidy surroundings reflected Colonel Vickers' efforts to create an amenable atmosphere.

6. Some Reflections on Pacifism

Gwenda Barer, the widow of Captain Robert Barer, the British Army doctor who was the first officer to enter Sandbostel Concentration Camp on its liberation, wrote to me after reading *Two Weeks in May 1945*:

> I appreciate specially your personal record of how you decided to be a conscientious objector and your description of the principles of the Society of Friends, which I admire very much. My husband and I came happily, from different origins, to a similar humanist and ethical standpoint which sustained us, though without faith, we felt we could not know about creation but were content to seek and do the best we could with the life we have. Robert did not think ethics had anything to do with religion, though historically most ethical systems developed in association with religions... As for pacifism, I could not sustain this in the face of Hitler and came to feel, then and now, that force is sometimes required. The trouble is, as seen so tragically in Kosovo, that force can never be 'surgical' – terrible horrors are always unleashed. In Oxford, an old and very famous Professor of Classics, turned out by the Nazis, lived in our house. His daughter had been in a concentration camp where she had a child who was removed from her. In 1945 she

found the child – pushed her in a pram across Europe, and arrived in Oxford. She remained a total pacifist – believed Hitler would have been toppled in the end! What do you think?

Replying to her thoughtful letter prompted me to look afresh at where I was in my thinking on these matters and to ask myself the question whether I would act the same today if a similar situation arose. Although I have written a little of how I became a conscientious objector in the Introduction to this book of my letters, and in the Prologue to *Two Weeks in May 1945*, it would still seem appropriate to reflect on my personal journey and how I view these matters today. I do not pretend to be any kind of expert and my views can only be those of an ordinary, but very concerned, newspaper reading layman, and I appreciate that what I have to say probably adds very little to current pacifist thinking which has been written about with more authority elsewhere*.

My background with Quaker parents and education at St Christopher School led me to pacifism (see pp.15–17). I had learnt from history how after the First World War the harsh reparations imposed on Germany led to hyper-inflation, vast unemployment, hunger and destruction of the economy, which created a situation where to many German people the ideas of the Nazi Party seemed a way out of their difficulties. I realised, however, that there were very many Christians who could fight as Christians, especially if moral issues were at stake. Many, I am sure, far better Christians in their daily lives than ever I had been, so I had to contend with the concept of a 'just' war. I had also read that several prominent people, including Winston Churchill†, had said that those who seek peaceful compromise may in the majority of instances be right, not only morally but also from a practical standpoint: but that the Christian must accept the fact that they live in a world where some aspects of Christianity are not fully accepted, and must therefore act in a sub-Christian way in order that Christianity itself may live. In such reasoning, pacifism becomes the vocation of a few, holding to a truth which could not be generally applied. It was a position I could respect, but not one I felt I could go along with, as it seemed to be a denial of what I understood as the very heart of Christianity. 'God is Love' made sense to me, and if the Quaker belief that there is 'that of God in every

---

* For example in John Lampen (ed.), *No Alternatives?* and Diana Francis, *Lessons from Kosova; alternatives to war* (for details see Bibliography, p.193)
† This idea was reiterated in Winston S. Churchill, *The Second World War*, 6 vols. (Cassell, 1948–1954)]

person' was true then it seemed to me there was no way that one could take another's life. In any situation what did love require of me? I became a conscientious objector.

Some sixty years on my basic thinking is much the same, although I feel my conviction has developed and I would wish to amend some of the Christian terminology. I am less innocent and more ready to understand why people feel that in some instances they have to resort to force, but am also more aware that this cannot be the right way. I know inwardly that the path of peace has to be the way forward, but still have great difficulty in trying to rationalise and articulate it to those who think otherwise; but then I recognise that it can be equally difficult to rationalise and articulate the spiritual concept of God.

This is not the place to catalogue and argue the details of all the many conflicts since the Second World War, but even a brief glance shows, it seems to me, that military force achieved few, if any, of the initial aims set at the outset. Incredible as it may sound, it would appear that too often a course of action was embarked upon which was based on misinformation and lack of a real understanding of the issues, and misguided 'interests' were allowed to influence the decisions.

Nothing can be achieved unless the building of trust begins and the violent tragedies of the past put into history. It can be done if the will is there. We have to take heart that after 30 years of bloodshed and bitterness the IRA in Northern Ireland did decommission their weapons, following the Good Friday Agreement. It took four and half years of talking to each other, trying to find common ground, trying to understand each others fears and aspirations, but despite many breakdowns, some trust finally began to emerge.

I would like to quote some comments of Diana Francis (*Lessons from Kosova* p.193) when she wrote that war in general has somehow

acquired a scarcely contested reputation for effectiveness. Nowadays it is presented as 'the means of last resort', what we turn to 'when all else fails' as if then we have something to rely on. Within the myth of war, to see injustice happening and not resort to war is to refuse to do what is right and bound to succeed. Maybe the myth takes its strength from our inability to accept realities of the human condition to bear the frustration of limited powers and the fact of vulnerability, just as to burn down a school or shoot some classmates may feel better than remaining powerless. How else can we explain that in the face of the predictable calamity that would be precipitated by the bombing campaign launched against

Serbia, the NATO governments went ahead? How else could it have seemed that making things unspeakably worse was better than doing nothing?

It seems to me that people always want immediate answers rather than looking at problems earlier before they reach crisis point and when the longer term solution might have been more acceptable. Once a crisis has been allowed to develop the options become very limited, and once war is unleashed there is a steady deterioration – what was once not even contemplated becomes the chosen course.

When I look back to the Second World War I wonder what would have happened if the whole country had done as I had done, and was without arms. I have no means of knowing; suffering there would have been, but perhaps no greater than that inflicted – much of it on others – in the chaos of war and its aftermath. Maybe a vast mass of people passively resisting the war makers would each gain strength and the endurance of common purpose that would wear out opposition or change its character. The campaigns of non-violence achieved independence for India, recognition of racial equality in the USA, and ended the Marcos dictatorship in the Philippines. In the end the extremes of communism in Eastern Europe collapsed and the Berlin Wall came down, apartheid was ended and democracy came to South Africa. I believe the view that modern war is now too terrible and destructive to contemplate, and is ruling itself out as a practical way of solving disputes, is very slowly, being more generally accepted. We shall probably have minor wars and international conflicts for many years to come, but there are signs of an increasing awareness and willingness to engage in mediation and conflict resolution, which is being studied as never before. The work to change the idea in people's minds that violence can ever be a solution to their problems and that there are alternatives, has to be increased. If this culture of peace could prevail then the rest will fall into place, although peaceful solution of our problems will never be easy, taking much time, patience, commitment and finance. In the culture of peace as war becomes unacceptable then the willingness to compromise will become an essential ingredient. As states realise it is no longer necessary to spend billions on armaments, the well-being of the world will benefit as funds are diverted to health, education and development.

So yes, I believe that I am still a pacifist and I hope I would be able to do it all again if the same situation arose. Part of our role is to maintain hope and I think there have to be pacifists to keep the concept of alternatives to war alive.

7. Epilogue

As described in *Two Weeks in May 1945* (p.66) the political prisoners found in Sandbostel Concentration Camp were transported there in cattle trucks from Neuengamme concentration camp in horrifying circumstances early in April 1945. Sandbostel came to be seen as an extension of the larger Neuengamme complex.

In May 2000 a new exhibition commemorating the liberation of both camps was opened at the Neuengamme Concentration Camp memorial site in Hamburg, organised by the Freundeskreis KZ-Gedenkstätte Neuengamme. Dr Hans Engel who had been invited to speak on this occasion wrote to me on his return to say that he had found it a most interesting and well organised event. Some 400 ex-prisoners and their relatives from all over Europe took part, and speeches were made by eminent presidents, mayors and professors. Wreaths were laid at the various camp sites and roses scattered in Lübeck Bay, where the RAF had sunk three ships drowning some 7,000 prisoners from Neuengamme, just three days before the armistice, mistaking the ships for military transports (see p.152, and *TWIM* p.106). The same evening the documentary film based on my book *Two Weeks in May 1945* was shown on Radio Hamburg TV.

In his speech Dr Engel described how as a British Army doctor he entered Sandbostel on his 29th birthday to find the most unbelievably, appalling conditions, an experience he has never been able to forget. He quoted the German Jewish poet, Heinrich Heine, who had written 100 years earlier,

When I think of Germany in the night,
all thought of sleep has taken fright

and went on to say even 55 years on, when occasionally he wakes in the night and remembers those terrible scenes, his peace has gone and he often cries quietly to himself. Dr Engel detailed much of the heroic work of rescuing and caring for those prisoners who could be saved. He expressed the hope that through the exhibition new generations can be informed, for those who have been murdered or made ill must be remembered for a long time. He closed his speech by quoting Schubert and Müller's 'Lindenbaum',

I am now many an hour
distant from that place,
and still I hear it murmuring –
you will find here your peace.

Bibliography

Readers wishing to know more about FAU work are referred in particular to two books: *Friends Ambulance Unit: the story of the FAU in the Second World War 1939–1946* by Tegla Davies (now out of print), and more recently *Pacifists in Action: the experience of the Friends Ambulance Unit in the Second World War* by Lyn Smith (1998). The story of the FAU Post-War Service can be found in *FAU: the Third Generation: The Friends Ambulance Unit Post War Service and International Service 1946-1959* by Roger Bush (1998). For the Friends Relief Service see *Quaker Relief* by Roger Wilson (1952, now out of print). The out of print books are often to be found in the libraries of local Quaker Meeting houses.

Quakers and wartime relief in Second World War:

Brenda Bailey, *A Quaker couple in Nazi Germany: Leonhard Friedrich survives Buchenwald* (York: Sessions, 1994).

Clifford Barnard, *Two Weeks in May 1945: Sandbostel concentration camp and the Friends Ambulance Unit* (London: Quaker Home Service, 1999).

Clifford Barnard, *Sandbostel revisited* (Welwyn Garden City: privately printed, 2001).

Roger Bush, *FAU: The Third Generation* (York: Sessions, 1998).

A. Tegla Davis, *Friends Ambulance Unit* (London: Allen & Unwin, 1947).

Tim Evens and Stuart Walters, *The Winford Team: a record of the life and work of a group of conscientious objectors engaged on orderly duties at Winford Hospital, Bristol, 1940–1944* (Bristol: privately printed, 1945).

Friends Ambulance Unit Chronicle (1939–46). The newsletter of the FAU, in Friends House Library.

J. Ormerod Greenwood, *The Quaker Tapestry: A celebration of insights* (London: Impact Books, 1990).

J. Ormerod Greenwood, *Quaker Encounters, vol.1 Friends and Relief: A study of two centuries of Quaker activity in the relief of suffering caused by war or natural calamity* (York: Sessions, 1975).

William R Hughes, *Indomitable Friend: the life of Corder Catchpool, 1883–1952* (London: Allen & Unwin, 1956).

Grigor McClelland, *Embers of War: Letters from a Quaker relief worker in War-torn Germany* (London: British Academic Press / I.B. Tauris, 1997). Grigor McClelland, a few years older than Clifford, was with 4 FAU in other parts of Germany.

Hans A. Schmitt, *Quakers and Nazis: inner light in outer darkness* (Columbia, MI: University of Missouri Press, 1997). Further references to William Hughes and Corder Catchpool.

Lyn Smith, *Pacifists in Action: the experience of the Friends Ambulance Unit in the Second World War* (York: Sessions,1998)

Roger C. Wilson, *Quaker Relief: an account of the relief work of the Society of Friends, 1940–1948* (London: Allen & Unwin, 1952).

Roger C. Wilson, *Authority, Leadership and Concern: A study in motive and administration in Quaker relief work* (London: Allen & Unwin, 1949; repr. Quaker Books, 2007).

Other books on Second World War relief and pacifism

Robert Barer (ed. Gwen Barer), *One Young Man and Total War – Normandy to Concentration Camp: A Doctor's Letters Home* (Durham: Pentland Press, 1998).

Ulrike Jordan, (ed.), *Conditions of Surrender: British and Germans Witness the End of the War* (London: Tauris Academic Studies, 1997).

F.A.E. Crew (ed.), *The Medical History of the Second World War: The Army Medical Services (Campaigns); vol.iv North-West Europe* (London: HMSO, 1962).

Lyn Smith, *Pacifists in Action: The experience of the Friends Ambulance Unit in the Second World War* (York: Sessions, 1998).

Peace

Diana Francis, *Lessons from Kosova; alternatives to war – the peace testimony in the 21st Century* (London: Quaker Peace and Social Witness, 2001).

John Lampen (ed.), *No Alternatives? Non-violent response to repressive regimes* (York: Sessions, 2000).

Brian Phillips and John Lampen (eds.), *Endeavours to Mend: perspectives on British Quaker work in the world today* (London: Quaker Books, 2006).

Other books mentioned in the text

Vera Brittain, *Humiliation with Honour* (London: Andrew Dakers, 1942).

Winston S. Churchill, *The Second World War, 6 vols* (London: Cassell, 1948–1954).

George Fox, *The Journal of George Fox*, ed. John Nickalls (Cambridge University Press, 1952; reprinted Philadelphia Yearly Meeting, 1997).

Han Suyin, *Destination Chungking* (London: Jonathan Cape, 1943).

Gordon Stifler Seagrave, *Burma Surgeon* (London: Gollancz, 1944).

Index

Lightning Source UK Ltd.
Milton Keynes UK
UKHW03f0224250418
321614UK00001B/50/P